TIME CHANGES IN THE WORLD

EXCEPT
CANADA
MEXICO
U.S.A.

1994
REVISED
EDITION

First Printing 1971
Twenty-first Printing 1994
ISBN: 0-86690-077-2

Published by:
American Federation of Astrologers, Inc.
PO Box 22040
6535 S. Rural Road
Tempe, AZ 85285-2040

Printed in the United States of America

TIME CHANGES IN THE WORLD
(Except Canada, Mexico, USA)

By

Doris Chase Doane

Books by Doris Chase Doane

Accurate World Horoscopes
Astrologers Question Box, Volume 1
Astrologers Question Box, Volume 2
Astrology As A Business
Astrology of Childbirth
Astrology Rulerships
Astrology: 30 Years Research
Contest Charts
Doane's 1981-1985 World Wide Time Change Update
Doane's 1986-1990 World Wide Time Change Update
Horoscopes of the U.S. Presidents
How to Prepare and Pass an Astrologer's Certificate Exam
How to Read Cosmodynes
Index to the Brotherhood of Light Lessons
Modern Horary Astrology
Positive Benefits of Astrology
Profit by Electional Astrology
Progressions in Action
Secret Symbolism of the Tarot
Tarot Card Spread Reader (with K. Keyes)
Time Changes in Canada and Mexico
Time Changes in USA
Time changes in the World
Vocational Selection and Counseling, Volume 1
Vocational Selection and Counseling, Volume 2
Zodiac: Key to Career (with C. Peel)

PREFACE TO 1982 REVISED EDITION

During the past seven years, since the first edition of this book appeared, there has been an unending process in my office of verifying place names and keeping up with the everchanging boundaries of some existing countries, as well as overabundantly creating new ones. The times being used all over the world have been in a constant state of flux, due to wars, changes in calendars, governments, energy crises, etc., as well as our own development of new information which has been heretofore unavailable.

It's been both an immense and fascinating project that has filled many filing cabinets with correspondence in a mind-boggling variety of languages. Without the wholehearted assistance of myriad serious astrologers from all over the world who dug out the facts locally, as well as those who helped me personally in correlating and translating this material, I doubt this new edition would have been possible.

To all those who gave so generously of their time and spirit, I say a heartfelt "Thank you!" Thank you not only for the help you have given me, but for the invaluable contribution you have made to those who will follow our footsteps in the art and science of astrology — so they may run where we walked and crawled.

We feel as if we've been put through the wringer of a crash course in geography. Not only have European boundaries bounced back and forth with alarming rapidity, but many of the far-flung former "Imperial" possessions have gained their independence from their old masters, and to celebrate, have changed their names. Africa and Asia are the "Ms.'s" of geography!

Old and new atlases have piled up as we diligently filled in the gaps in the old edition as well as adding the very latest information on these two continents. A thorough cross-reference has been established for names—used and changed during the past 150 years—of areas, countries, capitals, islands, etc. Now that so many new countries have emerged the maps of the world have completely changed—and are still changing. Today's newest atlas will be tomorrow's "old news."

These data were checked against the latest reference books for 1986, as well as for last century factors. The result is a listing that will not only find favor with the modern time researcher, but should also be invaluable to the historian seeking into the past.

This completely new edition has been greatly enlarged as well as updated. The information has been refined and improved upon in great detail. In addition, in order to make this book more easily used by a world-wide audience, many names are presented in several languages. Common names in use in most countries have been included.

The key to quickly locating the reference you urgently desire is to fully understand the presentation of this information. Every listing is based on six individual parts if the information is available:

1. Name
2. Location and capital
3. Adoption of calendar(s)

4. Time zone shifts
5. Daylight (Summer or War) time periods
6. Cross-reference

Unless indicated, no daylight saving time changes occurred during 1981-1990.

Doris Chase Doane
San Francisco, California
March 2, 1987

All changes through 1990 have been incorporated in this edition.

TABLE 1
CONVERSION OF LONGITUDE TO TIME

DEGREES						MINUTES	
°	h m	°	h m	°	h m	′	m s
0	0 00	60	4 00	120	8 00	0	0 00
1	0 04	61	4 04	121	8 04	1	0 04
2	0 08	62	4 08	122	8 08	2	0 08
3	0 12	63	4 12	123	8 12	3	0 12
4	0 16	64	4 16	124	8 16	4	0 16
5	0 20	65	4 20	125	8 20	5	0 20
6	0 24	66	4 24	126	8 24	6	0 24
7	0 28	67	4 28	127	8 28	7	0 28
8	0 32	68	4 32	128	8 32	8	0 32
9	0 36	69	4 36	129	8 36	9	0 36
10	0 40	70	4 40	130	8 40	10	0 40
11	0 44	71	4 44	131	8 44	11	0 44
12	0 48	72	4 48	132	8 48	12	0 48
13	0 52	73	4 52	133	8 52	13	0 52
14	0 56	74	4 56	134	8 56	14	0 56
15	1 00	75	5 00	135	9 00	15	1 00
16	1 04	76	5 04	136	9 04	16	1 04
17	1 08	77	5 08	137	9 08	17	1 08
18	1 12	78	5 12	138	9 12	18	1 12
19	1 16	79	5 16	139	9 16	19	1 16
20	1 20	80	5 20	140	9 20	20	1 20
21	1 24	81	5 24	141	9 24	21	1 24
22	1 28	82	5 28	142	9 28	22	1 28
23	1 32	83	5 32	143	9 32	23	1 32
24	1 36	84	5 36	144	9 36	24	1 36
25	1 40	85	5 40	145	9 40	25	1 40
26	1 44	86	5 44	146	9 44	26	1 44
27	1 48	87	5 48	147	9 48	27	1 48
28	1 52	88	5 52	148	9 52	28	1 52
29	1 56	89	5 56	149	9 56	29	1 56
30	2 00	90	6 00	150	10 00	30	2 00
31	2 04	91	6 04	151	10 04	31	2 04
32	2 08	92	6 08	152	10 08	32	2 08
33	2 12	93	6 12	153	10 12	33	2 12
34	2 16	94	6 16	154	10 16	34	2 16
35	2 20	95	6 20	155	10 20	35	2 20
36	2 24	96	6 24	156	10 24	36	2 24
37	2 28	97	6 28	157	10 28	37	2 28
38	2 32	98	6 32	158	10 32	38	2 32
39	2 36	99	6 36	159	10 36	39	2 36
40	2 40	100	6 40	160	10 40	40	2 40
41	2 44	101	6 44	161	10 44	41	2 44
42	2 48	102	6 48	162	10 48	42	2 48
43	2 52	103	6 52	163	10 52	43	2 52
44	2 56	104	6 56	164	10 56	44	2 56
45	3 00	105	7 00	165	11 00	45	3 00
46	3 04	106	7 04	166	11 04	46	3 04
47	3 08	107	7 08	167	11 08	47	3 08
48	3 12	108	7 12	168	11 12	48	3 12
49	3 16	109	7 16	169	11 16	49	3 16
50	3 20	110	7 20	170	11 20	50	3 20
51	3 24	111	7 24	171	11 24	51	3 24
52	3 28	112	7 28	172	11 28	52	3 28
53	3 32	113	7 32	173	11 32	53	3 32
54	3 36	114	7 36	174	11 36	54	3 36
55	3 40	115	7 40	175	11 40	55	3 40
56	3 44	116	7 44	176	11 44	56	3 44
57	3 48	117	7 48	177	11 48	57	3 48
58	3 52	118	7 52	178	11 52	58	3 52
59	3 56	119	7 56	179	11 56	59	3 56

Example: Convert S.T. Meridian 112E30 to hours and minutes East of Greenwich (0°).

112° - 7h 28m
 30' -   2m 00s add
 ─────────────────
7h 30m East of Greenwich

INTRODUCTION TO THE FIRST EDITION

Since the publication of *Time Changes in the USA*, I have had letters from all over the world urging me to write a book on time changes outside the USA. *Time Changes in Canada and Mexico* has been published. (Both are available from the American Federation of Astrologers, Tempe, Arizona.)

As records are incomplete, I have hesitated to do a world book. However, in 1969 I decided to at least compile the information I have been gathering since 1942 and make it available for researchers, students, and historians.

In view of this urgency, I must stress that the present work is incomplete and a presentation of the information available at this time. I would hope that readers having documented information which does not appear here would send it in for inclusion in future editions or supplements of this volume.

Scanning history reveals that a list of countries for each decade would change tremendously, especially during war periods. After jiggling the list several ways, I decided to list the countries as Eugene Dernay did in his *Longitudes and Latitudes Throughout the World.* (American Federation of Astrologers, 1948) To this I have added the names of sixty-nine new countries that have become independent since the beginning of World War II. An alphabetical order and cross reference has been employed to eliminate an index. This way the body of the book is an index in itself. Some countries have been called by many names. These are cross referenced.

Under the name of each country is given geographical location; the capital city(ies) (Longitudes and Latitudes were taken from Dernay for the most part); reference to past name or former possession or date of independence. Then follows adoption date of Gregorian Calendar, Standard Time Meridian (S.T.Meridian), Daylight Saving Time and Double Summer Time if observed.

See "Introduction" in *Time Changes in the USA* for information on converting Julian Calendar (Old Style—OS) to Gregorian Calendar (New Style—NS) for each century.

Dates are given "American style." That is, 9/25 equals the 25th day of the 9th month—September 25. **Readers abroad take note of this.**

Instead of using the names of Standard Time Zones (such as Central Europe Time or Middle Europe Time) or the letters for zones, I thought it more convenient and uniform to give the degrees (and minutes, if any) of the Standard Time Meridian (S.T. Meridian) to which the clocks in a given area were standardized.

By using Table 1, Conversion of Longitude to Time, the hours and minutes a Meridian is East or West of Greenwich can be quickly calculated.

For instance, the S.T. Meridian of Uruguay is 52W30 (Longitude). Consulting the table, look in the Degree column for 52. It equals 3 hours 28 minutes. Not look in the Minute column for 30. It equals 2 minutes. Add 3h 28m and 2m to find that Uruguay S.T. Meridian is 3h 30m West of Greenwich.

Some countries use the phrase Summer Time when their clocks are advanced. In this volume the term Daylight Saving Time is used to indicate one hour advance on the clock unless otherwise indicated.

When Double Summer Time (an extra hour advance, or two-hour advance from the S.T. Meridian) is observed, the dates appear in a section under the Daylight Time section of that country. Be sure to check it.

To assist our non-English-speaking friends, I am presenting the French, Spanish and German translations of this Introduction.

This volume, along with *Time Changes in the USA* and *Time Changes in Canada and Mexico* completes the trilogy of time books covering the world.

L'INTRODUCTION

Depuis la publication de *Time Changes in the USA* j'ai reçu des lettres du monde entier me demandant d'écrire un livre sur les changements de temps hors des Etats Unis. *Time Changes in Canada and Mexico* a subséquement apparu. (Ces deux livres peuvent se commander avec The American Federation of Astrologers, Tempe, Arizona, USA.)

Les renseignements ètant incomplets j'hèsitais devant un livre sur les changements de temps dans le monde. Néanmoins, durant l'année 1969 je decidais d'ordonner toutes les informations récoltées par moi depuis 1942 et de les offrir aux investigateurs, étudiants et historiens.

C'est donc là la raison pour laquelle cette présente oeuvre est seulement la présentation de l'information disponible aujourd'hui sur ce sujet. Si mes aimables lecteurs ayant des informations supplémentaires voulaient me les envoyer, je serais trop heureuse de les inclure dans les subsèquentes éditions. Examinant l'histoire mondiale on se rend compte que la nomenclature des nations change souvent, surtout durant les périodes de guerre. Apres avoir etudié plusieurs manières, je decidais d'adopter la nomenclature que Eugene Dernay employa dans son livre *Longitudes and Latitudes Throughout the World* (American Federation of Astrologers, 1948). A cette liste j'ai ajouté les noms de 69 nouvelles nations, nées depuis le commencement de la Seconde Guerre Mondiale. L'order alphabétique et de spéciales notes de référence ont été choisis pour éliminer un index. De cette manière le livre lui-même est une véritable table des matières. Les nations connues par différents noms sont également annotées; en dessous du nom de chaque nation, la location géographique est donnée ainsi que la (ou les) Capital. La longitude et la latitude indiquées sont presque toujours prises de Dernay; une référence du nom antérieur ainsi que de la nation qui eu le contrôle politique dans le passé et la date d'independence sont données.

Après vient la date d'adoption du Calendrier Grégorien, du Méridien Standard (S.T. Meridian), de l'heure d'été (Daylight Saving Time) ou de la double heure d'été (Double Summer Time) selon les cas.

Dans l'introduction de *Time Changes in the USA* on peut trouver l'information nécessaire pour convertir le Calendrier Julien (Old Style—OS) en Calendrier Gregorien (New Style—NS) pour chaque siècle.

Les dates sont données à l'américaine (American Style), 9/25 represente le 25ème jour du 9ème mois, c'est à dire le 25 Septembre. *Mes lecteurs à l'étranger doivent faire attention à ce détail.*

Au lieu d'employer les noms des Zones de Temps (S.T. Zone), comme Europe Centrale, etc., ou de designer ces zones par des lettres, j'ai pensé plus simple et uniforme de donner les degrés (et minutes, si celà était nécessaire) du Méridien Standard (S.T. Meridian) auquel les horloges d'une certaine superficie sont ajustées.

Usant la Table 1, Conversion of Longitude to Time, placée au commencement de ce livre on peut calculer facilement les heures et minutes auxquelles un méridien est placé, à l'Est ou Ouest de Greenwich.

Par exemple, le Méridien Standard (S.T. Meridian) d'Uruguay est 52W30 (Longitude). Consultant la table, cherchez 52 dans la colonne des degrés: égal 3 heures 28 minutes. Maintenant, cherchez 30 dans la colonne des minutes: égal 2 minutes. Additioner 3hs 28 min. et 2 min., le resultat est donc 3hs 30 min. à l'Ouest de Greenwich, position du Méridien Standard.

De nombreuses nations usent la phrase Heure d'Etè (Summer Time) quand leurs horloges sont avancées: dans ce livre, le terme Daylight Saving Time est employé pour indiquer une heure d'avance.

Quand la Double Heure d'Etè (une heure extra d'avance ou 2 heures sur le Meridien Standard) est observée, les dates paraissent dans une section spéciale, Daylight Time section, pour ce dit pays. Verifiez chaque fois.

Ce livre et ses compagnons, *Time Changes in the USA* et *Time Changes in Canada and Mexico* complètent la trilogie de livres dédie aux changes du temps pour le monde entier.

INTRODUCCION A LA PRIMERA EDICION

Desde la publicación de *Time Changes in the U.S.A.*, he recibido cartas del mundo entero, pidiéndome un libro sobre los cambios de hora fuera de los Estados Unidos. *Time Changes in Canada and Mexico*, ha sido publicado. (Estos dos libros pueden obtenerse por medio de The American Federation of Astrologers, Tempe, Arizona).

No poseyendo suficientes datos para un trabajo sobre los cambios de hora en todo el mundo, he titubeado escribir un libro que cubra el mundo entero. Sin embargo, en 1969, quise, por lo menos, compilar la información acumulada por mis esfuerzos desde el año 1942 y ofrecerla a investigadores, estudiantes e historiadores.

Debido a esta urgencia deseo dar énfasis al hecho de que la actual obra es incompleta y es sólo una presentación de la información disponible hasta el presente. Ojalá que aquellos lectores que posean datos que no aparecen en este libro, se sirvan mandármelos para incluirlos en ediciones suplementos subsiguientes.

Revisando la historia mundial, nos damos cuenta de que una lista hecha de los paises, por cada década, cambiaría enormemente, especialmente durante los períodos de guerra. Despues de haber hecho la lista de los paises en varias formas, decidi catalogarlos en la forma que lo hace Eugene Dernay, en su obra, *Longitudes and Latitudes Throughout the World*. (American Federation of Astrologers, 1948.) A esta lista añadi los nombres de 69 nuevas naciones que se formaron desde el principio de la Segunda Guerra Mundial. Los paises se han catalogado por orden alfabético, con las referencias necesarias, eliminando de esta manera el índice, ya que el libro en sí constituye un índice. Algunos paises se conocen por varios nombres, y en estos casos, hacemos la referencia necesaria.

Debajo del nombre de cada pais se da la siguiente información: La localidad geográfica, la capital, (las longitudes y las latitudes fueron tomadas generalmente de Dernay), y referencia al nombre que se usaba en el pasado, o antigua posesión o fecha de independencia. Seguidamente, se da la fecha en que se adoptó el Calendario Gregoriano, el Meridiano, según la Hora Standard y si se observaba la Hora de Verano o la Hora Doble de Verano.

Véase "Introducción" en *Times Changes in the U.S.A.* donde se da la información necesaria para convertir el Calendario Juliano al Calendario Gregoriano, para cada siglo.

Las fechas se dan usando el "estilo americano", es decir, 9/25 equivale al vigésimoquinto (25) día del noveno mes (Septiembre), es decir, Septiembre 25.

En vez de usar los nombres de las Zonas donde se usa la Hora Standard (tal como la Hora de Europa Central) o las letras que indican las zonas, estimé más conveniente y uniforme dar los grados (y minutos, si los hay) del Meridiano segun la Hora Standard, que servian de standard a los relojes en cada área.

Si se usa la Tabla No. 1, Conversión de Longitud a Tiempo, se puede calcular rápidamente las horas y los minutos que un Meridiano está al Este o al Oeste de Greenwich. Por ejemplo, el Meridiano según la Hora Standard de Uruguay es de 52.30 (Longitud). Consultando la Tabla, se busca 52 en la columna indicando los grados. Equivale a 3 horas, 28 minutos. Ahora busque el 30, en la columna de los minutos. Equivale a 2 minutos. Añada 3 horas y 28 minutos a 2 y hallará que el Meridiano Segun la Hora Standard de Uruguay está a 3 horas y 30 minutos al Oeste de Greenwich.

Algunos paises usan la frase "Hora de Verano" cuando adelantan el reloj. En este volumen, el término "Hora de Verano" se usa para indicar que se ha adelantado una hora al reloj, a menos que se indique otra cosa.

Cuando se usa Hora de Verano Doble (se adelanta una hora extra, o sea, dos horas a la Hora Standard Segun el Meridiano) las fechas aparecen debajo de la Seccion de Hora de Verano de ese pais. No deje de rectificar esto.

Para ayudar a nuestros amigos que no hablan inglés, se ha traducido la Introducción al francés, español y alemán.

Este volumen, junto con *Time Changes in the U.S.A.* y *Time Changes in Canada and Mexico*, completa la trilogía de las distintas horas del mundo.

DIE EINFÜHRUNG

Seit der Herausgabe von *Time Changes in the USA* erhielt ich Briefe aus vielen Teilen der Welt in welchen mir dringend empfohlen wurde ein Buch über Zeitwechsel ausserhalb den Vereinigten Staaten zu schreiben. *Time Changes in Canada and Mexico* ist bereits erschienen. (Beide Bücher sind erhältlich durch The American Federation of Astrologers, Tempe, Arizona, USA.)

Da es keine vollständige und richtige Informationen gibt, habe ich bisher davon abgesehen ein Welt Zeit-Wechsel Buch zu schreiben. Jedoch, im Jahre 1969, entschied ich mich, wenigstens an Hand der von mir gesammelten Informationen ein Buch zusammenzustellen, welches Forschern, Studenten und Geschichtswissenschaftlern behilflich sein wird.

Ich hoffe dass die Leser dieses Buches welche irgend andere urkundige Auskünfte haben, mir ihre Erfahrungen mitteilen würden damit ich dieselben in späteren Auflagen dieses Buches einschliessen kann.

Wenn wir die Welt Geschichte gründlich studieren, sehen wir klar und deutlich dass die Länderliste stetig wechselt, hauptsächlich in Kriegszeiten. Nach eingehendem Studium der Länderlisten, entschied ich mich, die Länder zu katalogisieren wie Eugene Dernay in *Longitudes and Latitudes Throughout the World* (American Federation of Astrologers, 1948). Ausserdem habe ich die Namen von 69 Ländern, welche zu Anfang des Weltkrieges selbständig geworden sind, eingeschlossen.

Alphabetische Ordnung und Kreuz-Hinweise sind angewandt um ein Inhaltsverzeichnis zu eliminieren, infolgedessen dieses Buch ist ein Inhaltsverzeichnis. Mehrere Länder haben verschiedene Namen: es wird kreuzweise darauf hingewiesen. Unter dem Namen jenes Landes ist seine geographische Stellung angegeben, der Name der Hauptstadt (Hauptstädte), Länge, Breite, sind fast alle dem Dernay Buch entnommen, Hinweis auf deren früheren Namen, früherem Besitzern oder Unabhängigkeits Datum.

Darauf folgt das Annahme-Datum des Gregorian Kalenders, Meridian Standard Zeit (Standard Time Meridian), Sommer Zeit (Daylight Saving Time) and Doppelte Sommer Zeit (Double Summer Time) wenn respektiert.

Für den Wechsel eines Julian Kalender-Datum (Old Style – OS) in ein Gregorian Kalendar Datum (New Style – NS) für jedes Jahrhundert, bitte lesen Sie die "Introduction" in *Time Changes in the USA*.

Daten sind im amerikanischen Stil angegeben. Beispiel: 9/25 ist der 25ste Tag im neunten Monat (September 25). *Ausländische Leser sind hierauf besonders aufmerksam gemacht.*

Anstatt Standard Zeit Zonen Namen (wie Central Europa, usw.) oder Buchstaben um die Zonen zu benennen, halte ich es für einfacher, die entsprechenden Standard Meridian Grade and Minuten zu geben.

Die Tabelle 1., "Conversion of Longitude to Time," am Anfang dieses Buch ist sehr nützlich um die Stunden und Minuten, von irgend einem Meridian Ost oder West von Greenwich, schnell auszurechnen. Zum Beispiel, der Standard Zeit Meridian in Uruguay ist 52W30 (Länge): siehe in der *Degree* Reihe für 52: ist gleich 3 Stunden 28 Minuten. Dann siehe in der *Minute* Reihe für 30: ist gleich 2 Minuten. Wir addieren beide und finden das Uruguay Standard Zeit Meridian ist 3 Stunden 30 Minuten West von Greenwich.

Mehrere Länder benutzen den Ausdruck Sommer Zeit wenn deren Uhren vorgestellt sind. In diesem Buch, benutzt man den Ausdruck "Daylight Saving Time" um eine Stunde vorgestellt zu zeigen. Wenn Doppelte Sommer Zeit ist beachtet (eine extra Stunde vorgerückt, oder zwei Stunden von Standard Zeit Meridian) die Daten erscheinen in dem Paragraph unter der Sommer Zeit (Daylight Saving Time) in jenem Land. Bitte Acht darauf geben.

Dieses Buch, zusammen mit *Time Changes in the USA* und *Time Changes in Canada and Mexico* vollendet die Trilogie der Zeit-Bücher für die Welt.

TIME CHANGES IN THE WORLD

ABYSSINIA See Ethiopia

ACORES See Azores

ADEN
Former British Colony and Protectorate on Arabian Peninsula
Capital: City of Aden   12N47   45E02

1931   Using S.T. Meridian 44E48 30", except Makalla which uses 33E45.
(Adoption date unknown)
1939   S.T. Meridian 45E00
No Daylight Saving Time

See also **People's Democratic Republic of Yemen**

ADMIRALTY ISLANDS   See New Guinea

AFARS AND ISSAS, FRENCH TERRITORY OF   See French Somaliland

AFGHANISTAN
Kingdom in Western Asia
Capital: Kabul   34N30   69E13

60E00 S.T. Meridian assigned in 1934, but not used. Time really not standardized. No DST

AFRIQUE DU SUD   See Union of South Africa

AFRIQUE EQUATORIALE FRANCAISE   See French Equatorial Africa

AFRIQUE OCCIDENTALE FRANCAISE   See French West Africa

AFRIQUE OCCIDENTALE PORTUGAISE   See Portuguese West Africa

AFRIQUE ORIENTALE ALLEMAND   See Belgian Congo and Tanganyika

AFRIQUE ORIENTALE ANGLAISE   See Kenya, Uganda and Zanzibar

AFRIQUE ORIENTALE ITALIENNE   See Italian East Africa

AFRIQUE ORIENTALE PORTUGAISE   See Portuguese East Africa

ALBANIA
A Balkan communist republic, located on the east coast of the Adriatic
Capital: Tirana   41N02   19E04

Albania (*continued*)
To   1914 Local Mean Time
      1914 Adopted S.T. Meridian 15E00

DAYLIGHT SAVING TIME OBSERVED

1940 4/1 - 1942 11/2 (+ 2 hr)   1979 5/1 - 9/30
1942 11/2 - 1943 3/29 (+ 1 hr)   1980 5/1 - 9/30

1981 4/26 - 9/30	1986 3/30 - 9/28
1982 4/18 - 9/30	1987 3/29 - 9/27
1983 4/18e - 9/30e	1988 3/27 - 9/25
1984 4/18 - 9/30	1989 3/26 - 9/24
1985 4/18e - 9/30e	1990 3/25 - 9/30

ALGERIA

Former French Colony in North Africa. Became independent July 5, 1962.
Capital: Algiers 36N47 3E04

1891	3/15	Adopted Local Mean Time of Paris 2E20
1911	3/11	0:01 am Adopted S.T. Meridian 0E00
1941		S.T. Meridian 15E00
1945	11/18	S.T. Meridian 0E00
1956	1/29	0 hr S.T. Meridian 15E00
1963	4/14	0 hr S.T. Meridian 0E00

DAYLIGHT SAVING TIME OBSERVED
(Begins 11 pm, ends 0 hr)

1922 3/25 - 10/8	1930 4/12 - 10/5	1937 4/3 - 10/3	1981 4/24 -10/24
1923 3/26 - 10/7	1931 4/18 - 10/4	1938 3/26 - 11/2	1982 4/25 - 10/23
1924 3/29 - 10/5	1932 4/2 - 10/2	1939 4/15 - 11/19	1983 4/29 - 10/27
1925 4/4 - 10/4	1933 3/25 - 10/8	1940 2/24 - 1945 9/16 year round	1984 4/28 - 10/26
1926 4/17 - 10/3	1934 4/7 - 10/7	1978 5/23 - 9/20	1985 4/28 - 10/27
1927 4/9 - 10/2	1935 3/30 - 10/6	1979 3/23 - 9/20	1986 4/27 - 10/26
1928 4/14 - 10/7	1936 4/18 - 10/4	1980 4/25 - 10/25	1987 4/26 - 10/25
1929 4/20 - 10/6			1988 4/24 - 10/30
			1989 4/30 - 10/29
			1990 4/29 - 10/28

ALLEMAGNE See Germany

ALOFI ISLANDS See New Caledonia

ALSACE-LORRAINE See France

AMATONGALAND See Union of South Africa

AMIRANTES See Seychelles

AMIRAUTE, ILES See Seychelles

AMIS, ILES See Tonga Islands

ANCHWEI See China

ANDAMAN ISLANDS
With Nicobar Islands, form a province of India, located in the Indian Ocean
Capital: Port Blair 11N42 92E46

1920 (circa)   Adopted S.T. Meridian 97E30
No Daylight Saving Time

ANDORRA
Principality in Pyrenees on border of France and Spain
Capital: Andorra la Vella 42N31 1E30

Observes S.T. Meridian 0E00

No Daylight Saving Time

Andorra	
1981 - 85	No DST
1986	3/30 - 9/28
1987	3/29 - 9/27
1988	3/27 - 9/25
1989	3/26 - 9/24
1990	3/25 - 9/30

ANGLETERRE   See Great Britain

ANGLO–EGYPTIAN SUDAN   See also Sudan
Former British possession in East Africa. Became independent January 1, 1956.

1931   Adopted S.T. Meridian 30E00 (date of adoption unknown)
No Daylight Saving Time

ANGMAGSSALIK   See Greenland

ANGOLA
Former Portuguese colony in West Africa. Became independent November 11, 1975
Capital: Luanda 8S49 13E14

To   1911   Local Mean Time of Luanda 13E14
1911   5/26   Adopted S.T. Meridian 15E00
No Daylight Saving Time

ANGUILLA ISLAND
British associated state in the West Indies
Capital: The Valley 18N13 63W04

To 1912   Local Mean Time
1912   3/2   S.T. Meridian 60W00
No Daylight Saving Time

ANJOUAN ISLANDS
French possession in Indian Ocean

S.T. Meridian 45E00

No Daylight Saving Time (assumed)

ANNAM   See French Indo-China

ANTIGUA
British associate state in the West Indies. Dependencies are Barbuda and Redondo Islands.
Capital: St. John's 17N06 61W51

To	1912	Local Mean Time
1912	3/2	S.T. Meridian 75W00

No Daylight Saving Time

ARABIE SAOUDITE See Saudi Arabia

ARCHIPELAGO OF COLUMBUS See Galapagos Islands

ARGENTINA
Republic in South America
Capital: Buenos Aires 34S36 58W27

1894	11/1	Local Time of Cordoba 64W11
1920	5/1	0 hr Adopted S.T. Meridian 60W00

DAYLIGHT SAVING TIME OBSERVED
(Changes at 0 hr)

1930 12/1 - 1931 4/1	1939 11/1 - 1940 3/1	1967 10/1 - 1968 4/7
1931 10/15 - 1932 3/1	1940 7/1 - 1941 6/14	1968 10/6 - 1969 4/6
1932 11/1 - 1933 3/1	1941 10/15 - 1943 8/1	1969 10/5 - 1976 4/4
1933 11/1 - 1934 3/1	1943 10/15 - 1946 3/1	*1974 1/23 - 5/1
1934 11/1 - 1935 3/1	1946 10/1 - 1963 10/1	1976 10/3 - Adopted year round
1935 11/1 - 1936 3/1	1963 12/15 - 1964 3/1	1981 10/4 - 1982 4/4
1936 11/1 - 1937 3/1	1964 10/15 - 1965 3/1	1982 10/3 - 1983 4/3
1937 11/1 - 1938 3/1	1965 10/15 - 1966 3/1	1983 10/6 - 1984 4/1
1938 11/1 - 1939 3/1	1966 10/15 - 1967 4/2	1984 10/7 - 1985 4/7
		1985 10/6 - 1986 4/6

*Add 1 more hour for Double Summer Time   1986 - 90 DST year round

ARMENIAN S.S.R. See Soviet Union

ARUBA
An island in the Netherlands Antilles
Capital: Oranjestad 12N33 70W06

1912	2/12	Local Mean Time of 67W30
1965	1/1	0 hr S.T. Meridian 60W00

No Daylight Saving Time

ASCENSION ISLAND See St. Helena

ASHANTI See Gold Coast

AUSTRALIA
Continent and British Commonwealth in South Pacific

PROVINCES

Canberra	Capital territory	35S17 149E08
1911 1/1	(Inception) Adopted S.T. Meridian 150E00

DAYLIGHT SAVING TIME OBSERVED
(Changes at 2:00 a.m.)

1917 1/1 - 3/25	1945 - 1970 Not observed
1918 - 1941 Not observed	1971 10/31 - 1972 2/27
1942 1/1 - 3/29	1972 10/29 - 1973 3/4
1942 9/27 - 1943 3/28	1973 10/28 - 1974 3/3
1943 10/3 - 1944 3/26	1974 10/27 - 1975 3/2

New South Wales Capital: Sydney 33S55 151E10

To 1895	Local Mean Time of Sydney 151E10
1895 2/1	Adopted S.T. Meridian 150E00 (including Broken Hill)
1896 8/23	Adopted S.T. Meridian 135E00 in Broken Hill only
1899 5/1	Adopted S.T. Meridian 142E30 in Broken Hill only

DAYLIGHT SAVING TIME OBSERVED
(Changes at 2:00 a.m.)

1917 1/1 - 3/25	1945 - 1970 Not observed
1918 - 1941 Not observed	1971 10/24 - 1972 2/27
1942 1/2 - 3/29	1972 10/29 - 1973 3/4
1942 9/27 - 1943 3/28	1973 10/28 - 1974 3/3
1943 10/3 - 1944 3/26	1974 10/27 - 1975 3/2

Northern Territory Capital: Darwin 12S28 130E49

To 1895	Local Time
1895 2/1	Adopted S.T. Meridian 135E00
1899 5/1	Adopted S.T. Meridian 142E30

DAYLIGHT SAVING TIME OBSERVED

1917 1/1 2:00 am - 3/25 2:00 am
1918 - 1941 Not observed
1942 1/2 2:00 am - 1942 3/29 2:00 am
1942 9/27 2:00 am - 1943 3/28 2:00 am
1943 10/3 2:00 am - 1944 3/26 2:00 am
1945 Discontinued

Queensland	Capital: Brisbane 27S28 153E02
To 1895	Local Mean Time of Brisbane 153E02
1895 1/1	Adopted S.T. Meridian 150E00

Canberra, New South Wales

1986 10/19 - 1987 3/15
1987 10/25 - 1988 3/20
1988 10/30 - 1989 3/19
1989 10/29 - 1990 3/18
1990 10/28 - 1991 3/4

1975 10/26 - 1976 3/7
1976 10/31 - 1977 3/6
1977 10/30 - 1978 3/5
1978 10/29 - 1979 3/4
1979 10/28 - 1980 3/2
1980 10/26 - 1981 3/1

1975 10/26 - 1976 3/7
1976 10/31 - 1977 3/6
1977 10/30 - 1978 3/5
1978 10/29 - 1979 3/4
1979 10/28 - 1980 3/2
1980   11/1 - 1981 3/1

Australia

1981 - 85 No DST in Northern Territory, Western Australia, Queensland

Rest of country:
1981 10/25 - 1982 3/6
*1982 10/31 - 1983 3/5
1983 10/30 - 1984 3/3
  and Broken Hill
1984 10/28 - 1985 3/2
  and Broken Hill
1985 10/27 - 1985 3/1
  and Broken Hill

*New South Wales extended daylight time for an extra month. Careful checking of times revealed three different times in some homes. Tasmania turned back its clocks on March 28th and New South Wales went back on April 4.

Broken Hill is a mining town in the middle of nowhere and has remained on South Australia time.

Queensland (*Continued*)

DAYLIGHT SAVING TIME OBSERVED
(Changes at 2:00 a.m.)

1917 1/1 - 3/25
1918 - 1941 Not observed
1942 1/1 - 3/29
1942 9/27 - 1943 3/28
1943 10/3 - 1944 3/26
1945 - 1970 Not observed
1971 10/31 - 1972 2/27
1973 Discontinued

1986 - 88 No DST
1989 10/29 - 1990 3/4
1990 10/28 - 1991 3/3

South Australia Capital: Adelaide 34S55 138E35
To   1895   Local Mean Time of Adelaide 138E35
1895 2/1   Adopted S.T. Meridian 135E00
1899 5/1   Adopted S.T. Meridian 142E30

DAYLIGHT SAVING TIME OBSERVED
(Changes at 2:00 a.m.)

1917 1/1 - 3/25
1918 - 1941 Not observed
1942 1/2 - 3/29
1942 9/27 - 1943 3/28
1943 10/3 - 1944 3/26

1945 - 1970 Not observed
1971 10/24 - 1972 2/27
1972 10/29 - 1973 3/4
1973 10/28 - 1974 3/3
1974 10/27 - 1975 3/2
1975 10/26 - 1976 3/7

1976 10/31 - 1977 3/6
1977 10/30 - 1978 3/5
1978 10/29 - 1979 3/4
1979 10/28 - 1980 3/2
1980 10/26 - 1981 3/1

Tasmania   Capital: Hobart 42S54 147E22
To   1895   Local Time
1895 9/1   Adopted S.T. Meridian 150E00

DAYLIGHT SAVING TIME OBSERVED
(Changes at 2:00 a.m.)

1916 10/1 - 1917 3/25
(Rural times from January to
March should be checked
carefully.)
1917 10/28 - 1918 3/3
1918 10/27 - 1919 3/2
1920 - 1941 Not observed
1942 1/1 - 1942 3/29

1942 9/27 - 1943 3/28
1943 10/3 - 1944 3/26
1945 - 1966 Not observed
1967 10/1 - 1968 3/31
1968 10/27 - 1969 3/9
1969 10/26 - 1970 3/8
1970 10/25 - 1971 3/14
1971 10/24 - 1972 2/27

1972 10/29 - 1973 3/4
1973 10/28 - 1974 3/3
1974 10/27 - 1975 3/2
1975 10/26 - 1976 3/7
1976 10/31 - 1977 3/6
1977 10/30 - 1978 3/5
1978 10/29 - 1979 3/4
1979 10/28 - 1980 3/2
1980 10/26 - 1981 3/1

Queensland, Victoria
1986 10/19 - 1987 3/15
1987 10/25 - 1988 3/30
1988 10/30 - 1989 3/19
1989 10/29 - 1990 3/18
1990 10/28 - 1991 3/17

Victoria   Capital: Melbourne 37S50 145E00
To   1895   Local Mean Time of Melbourne 145E00
1895 2/1   Adopted S.T. Meridian 150E00

Victoria (*continued*)

DAYLIGHT SAVING TIME OBSERVED

1917 1/1 0:01 am - 3/25 2 am	1945 - 1970 Not observed	1975 10/26 - 1976 3/7
1918 - 1941 Not observed	1971 10/24 - 1972 2/27	1976 10/31 - 1977 3/6
1942 1/1 2:00 am - 3/29 2 am	1972 10/29 - 1973 3/4	1977 10/30 - 1978 3/5
1942 9/27 2 am - 1943 3/28 2 am	1973 10/28 - 1974 3/3	1978 10/29 - 1979 3/4
1943 10/3 2 am - 1944 3/26 2 am	1974 10/27 - 1975 3/2	1979 10/28 - 1980 3/2
		1980 10/26 - 1981 3/1

Western Australia Capital: Perth 31S57 115E50

To   1895   Local Time
1895   12/1   Adopted S.T. Meridian 120E00

DAYLIGHT SAVING TIME OBSERVED
(Changes at 2:00 a.m.)

1917 1/1 - 3/25	1944 - 1973 Not observed
1918 - 1941 Not observed	1974 10/27 - 1975 3/2
1942 1/1 - 3/29	1976 Discontinued
1942 9/27 - 1943 3/28	

AUSTRAL ISLANDS See French Polynesia

AUSTRIA

A republic located in Central Europe
        Capital: Vienna 48N12 16E23

1583   10/16   Adopted Gregorian Calendar
To   1891   Local Mean Time
1891   10/1   S.T. Meridian 15E00 adopted by railroads but most towns and rural areas
                  continued on Local Mean Time
1893   4/1   S.T. Meridian 15E00 now used in some small towns
1910   5/1   S.T. Meridian 15E00 finally spread country-wide

DAYLIGHT SAVING TIME OBSERVED

1981 3/29 - 9/26	1916 4/30 11:00 pm - 1916 10/1 1:00 am
1982 3/28 - 9/25	1917 4/16 3:00 am - 1917 9/17 3:00 am
1983 3/25 - 9/29	1918 4/15 3:00 am - 1918 9/16 3:00 am
1984 3/31e - 9/29	1919 4/28 2:00 am - 1919 9/29 3:00 am
1985 3/31 - 9/28	1920 4/5 2:00 am - 1920 9/13 3:00 am
1986 3/30 - 9/28	1921 - 1939 Not observed
1987 3/29 - 9/27	1940 4/1 2:00 am - 1942 11/2 3:00 am
1988 3/27 - 9/25	1943 3/29 2:00 am - 1943 10/4 3:00 am
1989 3/26 - 9/24	1944 4/3 2:00 am - 1944 10/2 3:00 am
1990 3/25 - 9/30	1945 4/2 2:00 am - 1945 11/18 3:00 am
	1946 4/14 2:00 am - 1946 10/7 3:00 am
	1947 4/6 2:00 am - 1947 10/5 3:00 am
	1948 4/18 2:00 am - 1948 10/3 3:00 am

AUSTRIAN POLAND See **Poland**

AUTRICHE See **Austria**

AZERBAIJAN S.S.R. See **Soviet Union**

AZORES

Portuguese colony in North Atlantic
Capital: Horta 38N31 28W38

1912 1/1 Adopted S.T. Meridian 30W00

DAYLIGHT SAVING TIME OBSERVED
1916 3/1 11:00 pm - 1916 11/1 0 hr
1917 3/1 11:00 pm - 1917 11/1 0 hr
1918 3/1 11:00 pm - 1918 11/1 0 hr
1919 - 1940 Not observed
1941 4/5 11:00 pm - 1941 11/1 0 hr
1942 3/14 11:00 pm - 1942 4/25 0 hr
*1942 4/25 0 hr (duration date unconfirmed)
1945 - 1959 (Assumed but not verified, perhaps same as Portugal)

1960 4/24 - 10/30	1967 4/2 - 10/1	1974 4/7 - 10/6	1981 3/28 - 9/26
1961 4/2 - 10/1	1968 4/7 - 10/6	1975 4/6 - 10/5	1982 3/27 - 9/25
1962 4/1 - 10/1	1969 4/1 - 10/5	1976 4/4 - 10/3	1983 3/26 - 9/24
1963 4/1 - 10/6	1970 4/5 - 10/4	1977 4/3 - 10/2	1984 3/24 - 9/29
1964 4/5 - 10/4	1971 4/4 - 10/3	1978 4/2 - 10/1	1985 3/23 - 9/28
1965 4/4 - 10/3	1972 4/2 - 10/1	1979 4/1 - 10/7	1986 3/30 - 9/28
1966 4/3 - 10/2	1973 4/1 - 10/7	1980 4/6 - 10/5	1987 3/29 - 9/27
			1988 3/27 - 9/25
	*Add 1 more hour for Double Summer Time		1989 3/26 - 9/24
			1990 3/25 - 9/30

BAHAMA ISLANDS

British colony in Caribbean
Capital: Nassau 25N05 77W20

To 1912 Local Mean Time
1912 3/2 Adopted S.T. Meridian 75W00

DAYLIGHT SAVING TIME OBSERVED

1970 4/26 - 10/25	1974 4/28 - 10/27	1978 4/30 - 10/28	1981 4/26 - 10/24
1971 4/25 - 10/31	1975 4/27 - 10/26	1979 4/29 - 10/27	1982 4/25 - 10/30
1972 4/30 - 10/29	1976 4/25 - 10/31	1980 4/27 - 10/25	1983 4/29 - 10/27
1973 4/29 - 10/28	1977 4/24 - 10/30		1984 4/28 - 10/26
			1985 4/28 - 10/27
			1986 4/27 - 10/26
			1987 4/5 - 10/25
			1988 4/3 - 10/30
			1989 4/2 - 10/29
			1990 4/1 - 10/28

BAHRAIN

Former British protected state situated along the Persian (Arabian) Gulf. Became
independent August 14, 1971.

Bahrain (*continued*)

Capital: Manama 26N14 50E35

S.T. Meridian 60E00 observed in some parts. See **Saudi Arabia**

BAKER ISLAND See Gilbert Islands

BALAMBANGAN ISLAND See Malaysia

BALEARIC ISLANDS
Ibiza, Cabrera, Formentera, Mallorca (Majorca), Menorca (Minorca)

Time same as **Spain**

BALI ISLAND See Netherlands East Indies

BANGGI ISLAND See Malaysia

BANGKA ISLAND See Netherlands East Indies

BANGLADESH
Former East Pakistan achieved independence during the December 3–16, 1971
India–Pakistan war

Capital: Dacca 23N43 90E25

S.T. Meridian 90E00

BANKS ISLANDS See New Hebrides

BARBADE See Barbados

BARBADOS
Former British colony in the West Indies. Became independent November 30, 1966
Capital: Bridgetown 13N06 59W37

1924 Local Mean Time of Bridgetown 59W37
1932 Adopted S.T. Meridian 60W00

DAYLIGHT SAVING TIME OBSERVED

1978 4/16 - 9/30   1979 4/15 - 9/29   1980 4/20 - 9/25
1981 4/19 - 9/27
1982 4/18 - 9/26
1983 4/17 - 9/25
BARBARY See Libya   1984 4/22 - 9/23
1985 4/21 - 9/29
BARBUDA See **Antigua**   1986 4/27 - 9/28
1987 4/26 - 9/27
1988 9/24 - 9/25
BASUTOLAND See Union of South Africa and **Lesotho**   1989 4/30 - 9/24
1990 4/29 - 9/30
BATAVIA See Netherlands East Indies

BAVARIA (BAYERN) See Germany

BECHUANALAND See Botswana

BELGIAN CONGO

Belgian colony in Africa. June 30, 1960, became two independent countries called the Democratic Republic of the Congo. See **Congo** (Brazzaville) and **Congo** (Kinshasa).

Capital: Leopoldville 4S19 15E18

1912	1/1	Adopted S.T. Meridian 15E00
1920	4/25	Provinces east of Kalenga adopted S.T. Meridian 30E00;
		rest of country remained on S.T. Meridian 15E00
1935	6/1	Provinces divided into two time zones:

        S.T. Meridian 15E00 retained by western provinces of Coquilhatville, Leopoldville

        S.T. Meridian 30E00 adopted by eastern provinces of Castermansville, Elizabethville, Lusambo, Stanleyville

No Daylight Saving Time

BELGIQUE See **Belgium**

BELGIUM

Kingdom in Western Europe

Capital: Brussels 50N51 4E21

1582	12/25		10 days were dropped from Julian Calendar
1583	1/5		Adopted Gregorian Calendar, whose first day was 2/21/1583
1880			Local Mean Time of Brussels 4E21
1892	5/1	noon	Adopted S.T. Meridian 0E00
*1914	8/23	0 hr	Meridian shift to 15E00
1918	9/16	0 hr	Meridian shift to 0E00
*1940	5/20	3 am	Meridian shift to 15E00
1946	10/1	2 am	Meridian shift to 0E00
1953			Adopted S.T. Meridian 15E00

*In rural areas sometimes zone shifts were ignored, especially during the Occupation.

DAYLIGHT SAVING TIME OBSERVED

1916	4/30 11 pm - 10/1 1 am	1932	4/17 2 am - 10/2 3 am
1917	4/16 2 am - 9/17 3 am	1933	3/26 2 am - 10/8 3 am
1918	4/15 2 am - 9/16 3 am	1934	4/8 2 am - 10/7 3 am
1919	3/1 11 pm - 10/5 0 hr	1935	3/31 2 am - 10/6 2 am
1920	2/14 11 pm - 10/24 0 hr	1936	4/19 2 am - 10/4 3 am
1921	3/14 11 pm - 10/26 0 hr	1937	4/4 2 am - 10/3 2 am
1922	3/25 11 pm - 10/8 0 hr	1938	3/27 2 am - 10/2 2 am
1923	4/21 11 pm - 10/7 0 hr	1939	4/16 2 am - 11/19 0 hr
1924	3/29 11 pm - 10/5 0 hr	1940	2/24 11 pm - 5/19 3 am
1925	4/4 11 pm - 10/4 0 hr	1940	5/19 - 1942 11/2 3 am
1926	4/17 11 pm - 10/3 0 hr	1943	3/29 2 am - 10/4 3 am
1927	4/9 11 pm - 10/1 3 am	1944	4/3 2 am - 9/17 3 am
1928	4/14 11 pm - 10/7 3 am	1945	4/2 2 am - 9/16 3 am

Belgium (*continued*)
    Daylight Saving Time Observed (*continued*)

1929 4/21 2 am - 10/6 3 am	1977 4/3 2 am - 9/24 3 am	1981 3/29 - 9/26
1930 4/13 2 am - 10/5 3 am	1978 4/2 - 9/30	1982 3/28 - 9/25
1931 4/19 2 am - 10/4 3 am	1979 4/1 - 9/29	1983 3/27 - 9/24
1946 5/19 2 am - 10/7 3 am	1980 4/6 - 9/27	1984 3/28 - 9/23
		1985 3/31 - 9/28
		1986 3/30 - 9/28
		1987 3/29 - 9/29
		1988 3/27 - 9/25
		1989 3/26 - 9/24
		1990 4/1 - 9/30

BELIZE

British associate state on the east coast of Central America facing both the Caribbean Sea and Pacific Ocean

                    Capital: Belmopan 17N15 88W47

To   1912   Local Mean Time
1912 4/1   S.T. Meridian 90W00
             Daylight Saving Time perhaps the same as **British Honduras**

(Add 1/2 hour for DST)

1981 10/1 - 1982 2/13
1982 10/1 - 1983 2/12
1983 10/1 - 1984 2/11
1984 10/1 - 1985 2/9
1985 10/1 - 1986 2/8
1986 10/1 - 1989 2/8
1987 10/1 - 4/14
1988 10/1 - 1989 2/11
1989 10/1 - 1990 2/10
1990 10/1 - 1991 2/9

BELUCHISTAN See India

BENADIR See Italian East Africa

BENGAL NATION See Bangladesh

BENIN

Former overseas territory in French West Africa. Became independent August 1, 1960
                Capitals: Porto Novo 6N29 2E37
                          Cotonou   6N27 2E27

S.T. Meridian 0E00
See also **Dahomey**

BENKOELEN See Netherlands East Indies

BERMUDA

British colony in North Atlantic
                Capital: Hamilton 32N18 64W47

To   1930   Local Mean Time
1930 1/1   2:00 am   Adopted S.T. Meridian 60W00
             DAYLIGHT SAVING TIME OBSERVED
    1978 9/30 - 10/29   1979 4/29 - 10/28   1980 4/27 - 10/26

1981 4/26 - 10/24
1982 4/25 - 10/30
1983 4/29 - 10/27
1984 4/28 - 10/26
1984 4/28 - 10/27
1986 4/27 - 10/26
1987 4/5 - 10/25
1988 4/3 - 10/30
1989 4/2 - 10/29
1990 4/1 - 10/28

BESSARABIA See Romania, Soviet Union (Moldavian S.S.R.)

BHUTAN

Buddhist kingdom in eastern Himalayas
                Capital: Thimphu   27N37   89E52

Local Mean Time in use. However, India designated S.T. Merdian as 82E30

BIKINI See South Sea Mandated Territories

BILLITON ISLAND See Netherlands East Indies

BIRMANIE See Burma

BISMARCK ARCHIPELAGO See New Guinea

BOEHMEN See Czechoslovakia

BOHEMIA See Czechoslovakia

BOLIVIA
Republic in South America
Capital: Legal capital is where the
Supreme Court meets in Sucre   19S03   65W17
Rest of government located in La Paz   16S30   68W09

To   1932   Local Mean Time of La Paz   68W09
1932   3/21 0 hr Adopted S.T. Meridian   60W00

DAYLIGHT SAVING TIME OBSERVED
1931 10/15 0 hr - 1932 3/21 0 hr

BONAIRE
An island in the Netherlands Antilles
Capital: Kralendijk   12N10   68W17

1912   2/2   Local Mean Time of Kralendijk   68W17
1965   1/1 0 hr   S.T. Meridian   60W00
No Daylight Saving Time

BONIN ISLANDS See Japan

BORNEO See Netherlands East Indies and British North Borneo

BORNEO BRITAINNIQUE See British North Borneo

BORNEO HOLLANDAISE See Netherlands East Indies

BOSNIA See Yugoslavia

BOTSWANA
Former British protectorate (Bechuanaland) in South Africa. Became independent republic
September 30, 1966
Capital: Gaborone   21S13   27E31

S.T. Meridian 30E00
No Daylight Saving Time

BRAZIL

Republic in South America

Capital: Brasilia 22S54 43W15 (formerly Rio de Janeiro)

To   1914   Local Mean Time
1914   1/1 0 hr   Territory divided into four time zones:

Zone No. 1   Adopted S.T. Meridian 30W00
Fernando Noronha (a penal settlement) and Isle de Trindade (virtually uninhabited)

Zone No. 2   Adopted S.T. Meridian 45W00
Most inhabited zone. Contains Federal District (Brasilia)

Bahaia (Alagoas)	Paraibo
Ceara	Pernambuco
Espirito Santo	Piaui
Goioz	Rio de Janeiro
Maranhao (Sao Luiz)	Rio Grande do Sul (Porte Alegre)
Minas Gerais	Rio Grande de Norte
Pora (east of Pecuari, Jari, and Xingu rivers)	Sao Paulo
	Santa Catarina
Parana	Serggipe

Zone No. 3   Adopted S.T. Meridian 60W00
Amazonas (east of a great circle joining Tabatinga to Porto Acre and including those two towns). Mato Grosso. Poro west of the Pecuari, Jari and Xingu rivers

Zone No. 4   Adopted S.T. Meridian 75W00
Part of Amazonas not included in Zone No. 3 and territory of Acre

1943   10/1   Surrounding territory taken in and divided into Federal territories, viz: Amapa (previously part of Eastern Pora), Rio Branco (previously part of Eastern Amazonas), Guapore (previously part of Eastern Amazonas and Mato Grosso), Ponta Pora (previously part of Mato Grosso), Fernando Noronha and Iguassu (previously parts of Parana and Santo Catarina). Most of these areas are uninhabited.

1946   Territories of Iguassu and Ponta Pora restored to original states.

DAYLIGHT SAVING TIME OBSERVED
(Not observed in Zone No. 1)

1953 12/1 - 1954 2/28
1963 10/23 - 1964 12/8 *
1964 12/9 - 1965 3/1
1965 10/30 - 1966 3/31
1966 11/1 - 1967 3/1
1967 11/1 - 1968 3/1
1968 11/1 - 1969 3/1

* Observed in these states only:
Sao Paulo, Rio de Janiero, Guanabara, Minas Gerais and Espirito Santo.

1931 10/3 1 am - 1932 4/1 0 hr
1932 10/3 0 hr - 1933 3/31 0 hr (except Maranhao)
1933 - 1948 Same dates as above
1949 12/1 0 hr - 1950 4/16 0 hr
1950 12/1 0 hr - 1951 3/31 0 hr
1951 12/1 0 hr - 1952 3/31 0 hr
1952 12/1 0 hr - 1953 4/1 0 hr

1985 11/2 - 1986 3/1
1986 10/25 - 1987 2/14
1987 10/25 - 1988 2/7
1988 10/16 - 1989 1/29 (1)
1989 10/15 - 1990 2/11 (2)
1990 10/21 - 1991 2/17 (2)

(1) Except in the states of Acre, Amapa, Para, Roraima and Rodonia.

(2) Only in the states of Sao Paulo, rio de Janeiro, Guanabara, Minas Gerais, Espirito Santo, Rio Grande do Sol, Santa Catarino, Parana, Goias, Tocantins, Mato Grosso do Sol, Mato Grosso, Bahai, Sergipe, Alagoas, Pernambu. Paraiba, Rio Grande do Horte, Ceara, Piaoi e Naranh. Federal District and Ilhas Oceanicas.

BRAZZAVILLE See **Congo (Brazzaville)**

BRESIL See **Brazil**

BRITISH AFRICA See **Union of South Africa**

BRITISH BECHUANALAND See **Union of South Africa** and **Botswana**

BRITISH CAMEROONS See **Cameroon**

BRITISH CENTRAL AFRICA PROTECTORATE See **Nyasaland**

BRITISH EAST AFRICA See **Kenya, Uganda** and **Zanzibar**

BRITISH GUIANA
>   Former British colony in South America
>   Capital: Georgetown 6N48 58W10

>   To   1915 Local Mean Time of Georgetown 56W10
>   1915 3/1   S.T. Meridian 56W15
>   No Daylight Saving Time
>   See also **Guyana**

BRITISH HONDURAS
>   British Crown Colony on East Coast of Central America
>   Capital: Belize 17N30 88W12

>   To   1912 Local Mean Time
>   1912 4/1   Adopted S.T. Meridian 90W00

DAYLIGHT SAVING TIME OBSERVED
(Changes at 0 hr)
Not observed in Puertos Cortes. Rest of area ½ hour only

1918 10/6 - 1919 2/12	1933 10/8 - 1934 2/11
1919 10/5 - 1920 2/13	1934 10/7 - 1935 2/10
1920 10/3 - 1921 2/13	1935 10/6 - 1936 2/12
1921 10/2 - 1922 2/12	1936 10/4 - 1937 2/14
1922 10/8 - 1923 2/11	1937 10/3 - 1938 2/13
1923 10/7 - 1924 2/10	1938 10/9 - 1939 2/12
1924 10/5 - 1925 2/15	1939 10/8 - 1940 2/11
1925 10/4 - 1926 2/14	1940 10/6 - 1941 2/9
1926 10/3 - 1927 2/13	1941 10/5 - 1942 2/15
1927 10/2 - 1928 2/12	1942 10/4
1928 10/7 - 1929 2/10	1977 10/1 - 1978 2/11
1929 10/6 - 1930 2/9	1978 10/1 - 1979 2/10
1930 10/5 - 1931 2/15	1979 10/1 - 1980 2/9
1931 10/4 - 1932 2/14	1980 10/1 - 1981 2/14
1932 10/2 1933 2/12	

BRITISH INDIA   See **India**

BRITISH LEEWARD ISLANDS   See **Leeward Islands**

BRITISH MALAYA   See **Malaya**

BRITISH NEW GUINEA   See **Papua**

BRITISH NORTH BORNEO
> British protected state in East Indies
> > Capital: Sandaken   5N50   118E07

1904	Oct.	Adopted S.T. Meridian 120E00
1946		Labuan (see **Malaya**) incorporated into British North Borneo

No Daylight Saving Time

BRITISH SAMOA   See **Western Samoa**

BRITISH SOLOMON ISLANDS
> British Protectorate in South Pacific
> > Capital: Tulagi   9S05   160E09

> S.T. Meridian   165E00

No Daylight Saving Time

BRITISH SOMALILAND   See **Somalia**

BRITISH TOGOLAND   See **Gold Coast**

BRITISH VIRGIN ISLANDS   See **Virgin Islands**

BRITISH WEST INDIES   See **Bahamas, Barbados, Jamaica, Leeward Islands, Trinidad and Tobago, Windward Islands**

BRUNEI
> British Protectorate on Borneo
> > Capital: Brunei   4N54   114 E57

> S.T. Meridian   120E00

BUKOVINA   See **Romania**

BULGARIA
> Republic in Southeast Europe. November 1940, came under German control. 1944, withdrew from World War II, U.S.S.R. refused to recognize neutrality. Now a communist state.
> > Capital: Sofia   42N42   23E20

Bulgaria (*continued*)

1915	11/13	Adopted Gregorian calendar
To	1894	Local Mean Time of Santa Sophia Cathedral in Istanbul 28E58
1894	11/30	Adopted S.T. Meridian 30E00
1942	11/2 3am	S.T. Meridian 15E00
1945	4/2 3 am	S.T. Meridian 30E00

DAYLIGHT SAVING TIME OBSERVED

1919 - 1920	Used by railroads, not populace	1944 4/3 2 am - 10/8 0 hr	
1921 - 1942	Not observed	1979 4/1 - 9/29	
1943 3/29 2 am - 10/4 3 am		1980 4/1 - 9/27	
		1981 4/5 - 9/26	1986 3/30 - 9/28
		1982 4/4 - 9/25	1987 3/29 - 9/27
		1983 4/3 - 9/24	1988 3/27 - 9/25
		1984 4/1 - 9/29	1989 3/26 - 9/24
		1985 4/7 - 9/28	1990 3/25 - 9/30

BURGENLAND See Austria

BURMA

Republic (formerly British control) in Southeast Asia. Became independent January 4, 1948

Capital: Rangoon 16N48 96E09

(in hot weather season): Maymo 22N02 96E28

To	1920	Local Mean Time of Rangoon 96E09
	1920	S.T. Meridian 97E30

No Daylight Saving Time

BURUNDI

Kingdom in East Central Africa. Formerly southern part of **Belgian Congo**. Became independent July 1, 1962

Capital: Bujumbura 3S24 29E21

S.T. Meridian 30E00

No Daylight Saving Time

BURYAT–MONGOL See Soviet Union

BYELORUSSIAN S.S.R. See Soviet Union

CABRERO See Balearic Islands

CAICOS ISLANDS See Jamaica

CAMBODIA

Former French protectorate in Southeast Asia. Became independent November 9, 1953.
Changed name to the Khmer Republic in October 1970

Capital: Phnom Penh 11N33 104E52

1906	6/9	Local Mean Time 106E35
1911	3/11 0:01 am	S.T. Meridian 105E00
1912	5/1	S.T. Meridian 120E00

Cambodia (*continued*)
1931   5/1   S.T. Meridian 105E00
                              No Daylight Saving Time
         See also **French Indo-China**

CAMEROON, FEDERAL REPUBLIC OF
Former French and British Cameroons in West Africa. Became independent January 1, 1960.
The northern (British) section united with Nigeria October 1, 1961.
         Capital: Yaounde 3N51 11E32

To   1912   Local Mean Time
1912   1/1   Adopted S.T. Meridian 15E00
                      No Daylight Saving Time

CANARY ISLANDS
Spanish possession in North Atlantic, including Fuerteventura, Gomera, Grand Canary,
Hierro, Lanzarote, Palma, Tenerife
         Capital: Santa Cruz de Tenerife 28N28 16W15

1901   1/1   S.T. Meridian 15W00
1927   Divided into two provinces: Santa Cruz de Tenerife and Las Palmas
1940s   S.T. Meridian 0W00
                   DAYLIGHT SAVING TIME OBSERVED
         1978 4/2 - 9/30   1979 4/1 - 9/29   1980 3/30 - 9/28   DST Same as Spain

CANBERRA See Australia

CANTON ISLAND See Gilbert Islands

CAPE COLONY PROVINCE See Union of South Africa

CAPE OF GOOD HOPE See Union of South Africa

CAPE VERDE ISLANDS
Former Portuguese colony in North Atlantic. Became independent July 5, 1975.
         Capital: Praia 14N56 23W31

(Begins 1 AM, ends 0 hour)

1981 3/28 - 9/26	1986 3/30 - 9/28
1982 3/27 - 9/25	1987 3/29 - 9/27
1983 3/26 - 9/24	1988 3/27 - 9/25
1984 3/24 - 9/29	1989 3/26 - 9/24
1985 3/23 - 9/28	1990 3/25 - 9/30

1912   1/1   Adopted S.T. Meridian 30W00
                      No Daylight Saving Time

CAROLINES See South Sea Mandated Territories

CARRIACOU ISLAND See Grenada

CATALONIA Same as Spain

CAYMAN ISLANDS See Jamaica

CELEBES See Netherlands East Indies

CENTRAL AFRICAN PROTECTORATE   See **Nyasaland**

CENTRAL AFRICAN REPUBLIC
>   Formerly part of French Equatorial Africa. Became independent August 13, 1960
>   Capital: Bangui 4N21 18E35

>   1912 1/1 Adopted S.T. Meridian 15E00
>   No Daylight Saving Time

CERAM ISLAND   See **Netherlands East Indies**

CESKOSLOVENSKA   See **Czechoslovakia**

CEUTA   See **Spain**

CEYLON
>   Formerly British Crown Colony in Asia. Became independent February 4, 1948. On May 22,
>   1972 became the Republic of Sri Lanka
>   Capital: Columbo 6N57 79E53

>   To   1906 Local Mean Time of Columbo 79E53
>   1906 1/1 Adopted S.T. Meridian 82E30

>   DAYLIGHT SAVING TIME OBSERVED
>   1942 1/5 Time advanced ½ hour
>   1942 9/1 Time advanced ½ hour (making 1 hour)
>   1945 10/16 2 am Returned to Standard Time

CHAD
>   Formerly part of French Equatorial Africa. Became independent August 11, 1960.
>   Capital: Ndjamena 12N07 15E03

>   1912 1/1 Adopted S.T. Meridian 15E00
>   DAYLIGHT SAVING TIME OBSERVED
>   1979 10/14 - 1980 3/8

CHAGOS ISLAND
>   British possession in Indian Ocean

>   1907 1/1 Adopted S.T. Meridian 75E00
>   No Daylight Saving Time

CHANDERNAGOR   See **French Establishments in India**

CHANNEL ISLANDS   See **Great Britain**

CHATHAM ISLANDS
>   Dependency of New Zealand located about 400 miles east of the South Island
>   Capital: Waitangi 43S57 176E34

Chatham Islands (*continued*)
Through 1945   S.T. Meridian 172E30
1946 1/18   Adopted S.T. Meridian 180°E11'15", which is 45 minutes in advance of
New Zealand Standard Time (180E). Even though this appears to cross the
international dateline, it is used to calculate the hours east of Greenwich.
Daylight Savings Time observed on the same dates as New Zealand

CHEKIANG See China

CHESTERFIELD ISLANDS See New Caledonia

CHILE
Republic in South America
Capital: Santiago 33S27 70W40

To 1910   Local Mean Time of Santiago 70W40
1910   1/1   Adopted S.T. Meridian 75W00
1932   9/1 0 hr   Adopted S.T. Meridian 60W00

DAYLIGHT SAVING TIME OBSERVED
(Changes at 0 hr)

Santiago
1918 9/1 - 1919 7/2
1920 - 1926 Not observed
1927 9/1 - 1928 4/1
1928 9/1 - 1929 4/1
1929 9/1 - 1930 4/1

1930 9/1 - 1931 4/1
1931 9/1 - 1932 4/1
1977 10/9 - 1978 3/11
1978 10/15 - 1979 3/10
1979 10/14 - 1980 3/8

Valparaiso
1931 9/1 - 1932 4/1
1981 10/11 - 1982 3/13
1982 10/10 - 1983 2/12
1983 10/9 - 1984 3/10
1984 10/14 - 1985 3/9
1985 10/13 - 1986 3/8
1986 10/12 - 1987 3/14
1987 10/11 - 1988 3/12
1988 10/9 - 1989 3/11
1989 10/8 - 1990 3/10

1990 10/14 - 1991 3/9

CHINA, PEOPLE'S REPUBLIC OF
Located in the eastern part of Asia, occupying five time zones. Republic of China founded
January 1, 1912. Name was changed to People's Republic of China September 21, 1949.
Country composed of 22 provinces, including Taiwan, which is under dispute, 5 autonomous
regions, and 3 municipalities.
Capital: Peking 39N36 116E24

Provinces	*Capital*	*Latitude*	*Longitude*
Anhwei	Hofei	31N54	117E18
Chekiang	Hangchow	30N17	120E10
Fukien	Foochow	26N05	119E19
Heilungkiang	Harbin	45N47	126E39
Honan	Chengchow	34N48	113E39
Hopei	Tientsin	39N08	117E12
Hunan	Changsha	28N12	112E59
Hupei	Wuhan	30N23	114E54
Kansu	Lanchow	36N03	103E41

China (*continued*)

Provinces	Capital	Latitude	Longitude
Kiangsi	Nanchang	28N40	115E53
Kiangsu	Nanking	32N03	118E48
Kirin	Changchun	43N54	125E20
Kwantung	Canton	23N07	113E16
Kweichow	Kweiyang	26N35	106E13
Liaoning	Mukden	41N48	113E26
Shansi	Taiyuen	37N55	112E30
Shantung	Tsinan	36N40	116E57
Shensi	Sian	34N16	108E34
Szechwan	Chengtu	30N40	104E04
Taiwan (See also **Taiwan**)	T'aipei	25N00	121E40
Tsinghai	Sining	36N37	101E49
Yunnan	Kunming	25N04	102E41

Autonomous Regions			
Inner Mongolia	Huhehot	40N51	111E40
Kwangsi–Chuang	Nanning	28N48	108E18
Ningsia–Hui	Yinchuan	38N30	106E18
Sinkiang–Uighur	Urumchi	43N48	87E36
Tibet–Chamdo	Lhasa	29N43	91E11

Municipalities		Latitude	Longitude
Peking		39N36	116E24
Shanghai		31N14	121E30
Tientsin		39N08	117E12

1912 2/12 Adopted Gregorian calendar. Republic of China founded.

1903 1/1 S.T. Meridian 120E00 observed on east coast only in principal cities such as Tientsin. No Standard Time observed in interior of China until 1928. Even after that year, sundials continued in use in the interior. In later years, time was telegraphed once a day to the interior, and in some places a gun was fired at noon.

1904 10/30 Canton, Hong Kong, Kongmoon, Macau, Swatow, Samshui, Wechow adopted S.T. Meridian 120E00.

1904 12/1 Chosen (now Korea), Manchuria adopted S.T. Meridian 135E00.

1905 8/1 Shanhai, Shuntung (Chinese Customs only) adopted S.T. Meridian 120E00.

1905 8/1 Hoichow, Lungchow, Pakoi adopted S.T. Meridian 105E00.

1928 China divided into five (5) time zones as follows:

China (*continued*)

TIME ZONES IN CHINA

Chang Pe Zone No. 1	127E30 to 120E00	S.T. Meridian 127E30

Chekiang	Manchuria
Chosen	Taiwan
Heilungkiang	Shanghai
Kirin	

Chung Yuau Zone No. 2	120E00 to 105E00	S.T. Meridian 120E00

Anhwei	Liaoning
Chekiang	Shansi
Fukien	Shantung
Honan	Shensi
Hopei	Inner Mongolia
Hunan	Kwangsi–Chuang
Hupei	Ningsia–Hui
Kiangsi	Pechili
Kiangsu	Peking
Kweichow	Tientsin

Lung Shu Zone No. 3	105E00 to 90E00	S.T. Meridian 105E00

Hainan Islands	Szechwan
Kansu	Tsinghai
Kwangtung (except Yatung)	Yunnan
Suchwan	Tibet–Chamdo

Hui Chang Zone No. 4	90E00 to 82E30	S.T. Meridian 90E00

Sinkiang–Uighur	Yatung

Kunlun Zone No. 5	82E30 to Eastward	S.T. Meridian 82E30

Sinkiang	Tibet

1932 3/1 10 am Chosen adopted S.T. Meridian 135E00.
1932 3/1 10 am Heilungkiang, Jehol, Kiangsu, Kirin, Liaoning, Manchuria adopted S.T. Meridian 120E00.

DAYLIGHT SAVING TIME OBSERVED

1940 6/3 Observed by International Settlement and French Concession in Shanghai
1941 3/16 0 hr Observed in Shanghai and Central China (including Hankow, Hangchoo, Nanking and Soochow)
1960 - 1977 Not observed

CHINA, REPUBLIC OF See **Taiwan**

CHINESE TURKESTAN See China

CHOSEN See Korea

CHUNG-HUA MIN-KUO See China

CHUVASH S.S.R. See Soviet Union

CHYPRE See Cyprus

COLUMBIA
Republic in South America
Capital: Bogota 4N40 74W05

1884 3/13 U.S. placed country on S.T. Meridian 75W00, but Local Mean Time of Bogota
was used: 74W05
1914 11/23 Adopted S.T. Meridian 75W00
No Daylight Saving Time

COMORO ISLANDS
Former French mandate in Indian Ocean. Became independent July 6, 1975.
Capital: Moronia 11S41 43E16

1911 7/1 Adopted S.T. Meridian 45E00
No Daylight Saving Time

CONFEDERATION SUISSE See Switzerland

CONGO
Former Belgian Congo and French Equatorial Africa

1912 1/1 Adopted S.T. Meridian 15E00
1935 6/1 Belgian Congo divided its provinces into two zones:

S.T. Meridian 15E00 adopted by *Western Provinces:*
Coquilhatville and Leopoldville
S.T. Meridian 30E00 adopted by *Eastern Provinces:* Costermansville,
Elizabethville, Lusambo and Stanleyville
1960 (after) See **Congo** (Brazzaville) and **Congo** (Kinshasa)
No Daylight Saving Time

CONGO (Brazzaville)
Became independent August 15, 1960
Capital: Brazzaville 4S17 15E14

Observes S.T. Meridian 15E00
No Daylight Saving Time

CONGO (Kinshasa)
　　Became independent June 30, 1960
　　　　　　　　　　Capital:　Kinshasa   4S19   15E18

　　Observes S.T. Meridian 15E00
　　　　　　　　　　　　No Daylight Saving Time

CONGO BELGE   See **Belgian Congo**

CONGO MOYEN   See **Congo** (Brazzaville)

CONGRESS POLAND   See **Poland**

COOK ISLANDS
　　Dependency of New Zealand in South Pacific
　　　　　　　　Capital:　Avarua   21S12   159W46

　　Observes S.T. Meridian 157W30
　　　　　　　　　　DAYLIGHT SAVING TIME OBSERVED
　　　　　　　　　1979 10/7 - 1980 3/30

1981 10/25 - 1982 3/6	1986 10/26 - 1987 3/17
1982 10/31 - 1983 3/5	1987 10/25 - 1988 3/5
1983 10/30 - 1984 3/3	1988 10/30 - 1989 3/4
1984 10/28 - 1985 3/2	1989 10/27 - 1990 3/3
1985 10/27 - 1986 3/1	1990 10/28 - 1991 3/2

COREE   See **Korea**

CORSICA   See **France**

COSTA RICA
　　Republic in Central America
　　　　　　　　Capital:　San Jose   9N56   84W05

　　To 1921　　　Local Mean Time of San Jose 84W05
　　1921   1/15　Adopted S.T. Meridian 90W00

　　　　　　　　DAYLIGHT SAVING TIME OBSERVED
　　　　　1979 2/25 - ?　　　　　　　1980 2/24 - 6/1

COTE D'IVOIRE   See **French West Africa**

COTE D'OR   See **Gold Coast Colony**

COTE FRANCAISE DES SOMALIS   See **French Somaliland**

CRETE   See **Greece**

CRIMEA   See **Soviet Union**

CROATIA   See **Yugoslavia**

CUBA
　　Republic located in Greater Antilles
　　　　　　　　Capital:　Havana (Habana)   23N08   82W24

　　To 1925　　　Local Mean Time of Havana 82W24
　　1925   7/19　Noon, Adopted S.T. Meridian 75W00

Cuba (*continued*)

DAYLIGHT SAVING TIME OBSERVED
(Changes at 0 hr)

1928 6/10 - 10/10	1970 4/26 - 10/25	1981 5/10 - 10/10
1929 - 1939 Not observed	1971 4/25 - 10/30	1982 5/9 - 10/9
1940 6/2 - 9/1	1972 4/30 - 10/8	1983 5/8 - 10/8
1941 6/1 - 9/7	1973 4/29 - 10/8	1984 5/13 - 10/13
1942 6/7 - 9/6	1974 4/28 - 10/8	1985 5/12 - 10/12
1943 - 1964 Not observed	1975 4/27 - 10/26	1986 3/16 - 10/11
1965 6/1 - 9/30	1976 4/25 - 10/31	1987 3/15 - 10/10
1966 5/29 - 10/2	1977 4/24 - 10/30	1988 3/20 - 10/8
1967 4/8 - 9/10	1978 5/7 - 10/8	1989 3/19 - 10/7
1968 4/14 - 9/8	1979 3/18 - 10/14	1990 3/18 - 10/6
1969 4/27 - 10/26	1980 3/16 - 10/12	

CURACAO
Islands off the coast of Venezuela in the Netherlands Antilles

1912   2/12   S.T. Meridian 67W30
1965   1/1   0 hr S.T. Meridian 60W00
                        No Daylight Saving Time

CYPRUS
Former British possession in Mediterranean. Now Republic of Cyprus.   Became independent
August 16, 1960

Capital: Nicosia 35N12 33E22	1981 3/29 - 9/26
	1982 3/28 - 9/25
	1983 3/27 - 9/24
1921 11/24 S.T. Meridian 30E00	1984 3/25 - 9/29
	1985 3/31 - 9/28
No Daylight Saving Time	1986 3/30 - 9/28
	1987 3/29 - 9/27
	1988 3/27 - 9/25
	1989 3/26 - 9/24
	1990 3/25 - 9/30

CYROT-TURA AREA   See Soviet Union

CZECHOSLOVAKIA
Republic in Central Europe. Now a communist state
            Capital: Praha (Prague) 50N05 14E26

To 1891   Local Mean Time of Prague 14E26
1891   10/1   Adopted S.T. Meridian 15E00

DAYLIGHT SAVING TIME OBSERVED

1916 4/30 11 pm - 1916 10/1 1 am	1943 3/29 2 am - 1943 10/4 3 am
1917 4/16 2 am - 1917 9/17 3 am	1944 4/3 2 am - 1944 10/2 3 am
1918 4/15 2 am - 1918 9/16 3 am	1945 4/2 2 am - 1946 11/18 3 am
1919 - 1939 Not observed	1979 3/30 - 9/27
1940 4/1 2 am - 1942 11/2 3 am	1980 3/30 - 9/27

(Begins at 0 hour, ends 1 AM)

1981 3/29 - 9/27	1986 3/30 - 9/28
1982 3/28 - 9/26	1987 3/29 - 9/27
1983 3/27 - 9/25	1988 3/27 - 9/25
1984 3/25 - 9/30	1989 3/26 - 9/24
1985 3/31 - 9/29	1990 3/25 - 9/30

DAHOMEY

Formerly a province in French Equatorial Africa (Soudan). Became independent August 1, 1960. In 1961 Sao Joao Batista de Ajuda, former Portuguese Overseas Territory, united with Dahomey. Changed name to the Republic of Benin.

Capital: Porto Novo 6N29 2E37

1912	1/1	0 hr	Adopted S.T. Meridian 0E00
1934	2/26	0 hr	Adopted S.T. Meridian 15E00

No Daylight Saving Time

DAITO ISLANDS See Japan

DALMATIA See Yugoslavia

DAMAN See Portuguese India

DAMARALAND See Union of South Africa

DANEMARK See Denmark

DANGER ISLANDS

Dependency of New Zealand in South Pacific

Capital: Pukapuka 10S53 165W49

S.T. Meridian 165W00

DANZIG

Seaport on the southern shore of the Baltic Sea

Capital: Danzig 54N21 18E39

1893	4/1	S.T. Meridian 15E00
1945		S.T. Meridian 30E00

No Daylight Saving Time

DARDANELLES See Turkey

DENMARK

Kingdom in Northern Europe

Capital: Copenhagen 55N41 12E35

1582	10/15 (NS)	Adopted Gregorian calendar
To 1894		Local Mean Time
1894	1/1	Adopted S.T. Meridian 15E00

DAYLIGHT SAVING TIME OBSERVED

1916 5/14 11 pm - 10/1 0 hr   (Begins 2 AM, ends 3 AM)
1940 - 1945 Same as Germany
1980 4/6 2 am - 9/28 3 am

1981 3/29 - 9/26	1986 3/30 - 9/28
1982 3/28 - 9/25	1987 3/29 - 9/27
1983 3/27 - 9/24	1988 3/27 - 9/25
1984 3/28 - 9/23	1989 3/26 - 9/24
1985 3/31 - 9/28	1990 3/25 - 9/30

DEUTSCHLAND See Germany

DIGUEL See Netherlands East Indies

DINDINGS See Malaya

DIU See Portuguese India

DJAWA See Java

DJIBOUTI
Formerly French Somaliland in East Africa situated at the Bab el Mandeb, at the mouth of the Red Sea. Became independent June 27, 1977
Capital: Djibouti 11N36 43E07

S.T. Meridian 45E00

DOBRUDJA See Romania

DODECANESE ISLANDS See Greece

DOMINICA
A British associate state in the Windward Islands
Capital: Roseau 15N18 61W24

To 1911   Local Mean Time
1911 7/1 0:01 am S.T. Meridian 60W00
No Daylight Saving Time

DOMINICAN REPUBLIC
Located in the Greater Antilles
Capital: Santo Domingo 18S29 69W53

To 1933   Adoption date unconfirmed. S.T. Meridian 70W00
1933   4/1   Noon, adopted S.T. Meridian 75W00

DAYLIGHT SAVING TIME OBSERVED

Add 1 hr:	Add ½ hr:	
1966 10/30 - 1967 2/28	1971 10/31 - 1972 1/21	1981 10/25 - 1982 1/21
	1972 10/29 - 1973 1/21	1982 10/24 - 1983 1/21
	1973 10/27 - 1974 1/21	1983 10/23 - 1984 1/21
Add ½ hr:	1974 10/27 - 1975 1/21	1984 10/28 - 1985 1/21
1969 10/26 - 1970 2/21	1975 10/26 - 1976 1/21	1985 10/27 - 1986 1/21
1970 10/25 - 1971 1/20	1976 10/31 - 1977 1/21	1986 10/26 - 1987 1/21
		1987 10/25 - 1988 1/21
		1988 10/30 - 1989 1/21
		1989 10/29 - 1990 1/21
		1990 10/28 - 1991 1/21

DUTCH EAST INDIES See Netherlands East Indies

DUTCH GUIANA See Surinam

DUTCHLAND   See Netherlands

DUTCH WEST INDIES   See Netherlands West Indies

EAST AFRICAN PROTECTORATE   See Kenya

EASTER ISLAND
Chile possession in South Atlantic
Capital: Hanga Roa   27S09   109W26

S.T. Meridian 105W00

DAYLIGHT SAVING TIME OBSERVED

1977	10/9 - 1978	3/11	1979 10/14 - 1980 3/9	
1978	10/15 - 1979	3/10	1980 10/12 - 1981 3/8	
			1981 10/11 - 1982 3/13	
			1982 10/10 - 1983 3/12	
			1983 10/13 - 1984 3/9	
			1984 10/12 - 1985 3/9	
			1985 10/13 - 1986 3/8	

EASTERN NIGER   See Niger

EAST GERMANY   See Germany, East

EAST PAKISTAN   See Bangladesh and Pakistan

EAST PRUSSIA   See Germany, Poland and Soviet Union (R.S.S.F.R.)

1986 10/26 - 1987 3/7
1987 10/25 - 1988 3/12
1988 10/30 - 1989 3/11
1989 10/29 - 1990 3/10
1990 10/28 - 1991 3/9

ECOSSE   See Great Britain (Scotland)

ECUADOR
Republic in South America
Capital: Quito   0S13   78W30

Formerly observed Local Mean Time of Quito 78W30
By 1931, observed S.T. Meridian 75W00 (adoption date uncertain)
No Daylight Saving Time

EGYPT
Formerly a kingdom. Now a republic in Africa
Capital: Cairo   30N03   31E15

1900   10/1   S.T. Meridian 30E00

Egypt (*continued*)

DAYLIGHT SAVING TIME OBSERVED

To 1939 No Daylight Saving Time	1966 5/1 - 9/30	1981 - 82 No DST
1940 - 1945 Observed Daylight	1967 5/1 - 10/1	1983 5/1 - 9/30
Saving Time each year	1968 5/1 - 10/1	1984 5/1 - 9/30
perhaps 4/15 - 9/5.	1969 5/1 - 10/1	1985 5/1 - 9/30
(Unconfirmed)	1970 5/1 - 10/1	1986 5/1 - 9/30
1946 - 1959 No information	1971 5/1 - 10/1	1987 5/1 - 9/30
1960 5/1 - 9/30	1972 5/1 - 10/1	1988 5/1 - 9/30
1961 5/1 - 9/30	1973 5/1 - 10/1	1989 5/1 - 9/30
1962 5/1 - 9/30	1974 5/1 - 10/1	1990 5/1 - 9/30
1963 5/1 - 9/30	1975 5/1 - 10/1	
1964 5/1 - 9/30	1976 5/1 - 10/1	
1965 5/1 - 9/30	1977 5/1 - 10/1	

EGYPTIAN SUDAN   See Anglo–Egyptian Sudan

EIRE (Ireland)
Free state in British Commonwealth. Located in Atlantic Ocean west of England
Capital: Dublin 53N20 6W15

			DST		
			1981 3/29 - 10/24	1986 3/30 - 10/26
1752	9/14		Adopted Gregorian calendar (NS)	1982 3/28 - 10/23	1987 3/29 - 10/25
1880	1/1		Local Mean Time of Dublin 6W15	1983 3/25 - 10/27	1988 3/27 - 10/30
1916	10/1		Adopted S.T. Meridian 0W00	1984 3/31 - 10/26	1989 3/26 - 10/29
1968	2/18	2 am	Adopted S.T. Meridian 15E00	1985 3/31 - 10/24	1990 3/25 - 9/30
1972	11/1	0 hr	Reverted to S.T. Meridian 0W00		

See also Northern Ireland (Ulster) under **Great Britain**

DAYLIGHT SAVING TIME OBSERVED
Same dates as **Great Britain** (see)
except in 1945 when DST was continued through
until October 6, 1946.

ELLICE, ELLIS ISLANDS   See **Tuvalu**

EL SALVADOR
Republic in Central America
Capital: San Salvador 13N41 89W12

To 1921   Local Mean Time of San Salvador 89W12
1921   1/1   S.T. Meridian 90W00
No Daylight Saving Time

ELSASS–LOTHRINGEN   See **France** or **Germany**

ENDERBURY ISLAND   See **Gilbert Islands**

ENGLAND See Great Britain

ENIWETOK See South Seas Mandated Territories

EQUATEUR See Ecuador

EQUATORIAL GUINEA
Formerly Spanish Guinea in West Africa. Fernando PO and Rio Muni joined and became independent October 12, 1968.
Capital: Malabo 3N45 8E47

1912 1/1 Adopted S.T. Meridian 0E00
No Daylight Saving Time

ERITREA
Former Italian colony in East Africa, now part of Ethiopia
Capital: Asmara 15N21 38E56

S.T. Meridian 45E00 since at least 1931. Adoption date unconfirmed.
No Daylight Saving Time

ERYTHREE See Eritrea

ESPAGNE See Spain

ESPANA See Spain

ESTONIA
Former republic in Europe. Now Estonian S.S.R. (see **Soviet Union**)
Capital: Tallinn 59N26 24E43

To 1921   Local Mean Time of Tallinn 24E43
1921   5/1   Adopted S.T. Meridian 30E00
1942 - 1944   Same as Germany
No Daylight Saving Time

ETABLISSEMENTS FRANCAISE DANS L'INDE See French Establishments in India

ETABLISSEMENTS FRANCAISE DE L'OCEANIE See French Polynesia

ETAH See Greenland

ETAT DE LA CITE DU VATICAN See Vatican City State

ETAT LIBRE D'IRLANDE See Eire

ETHIOPIA
Monarchy in East Africa. Monarchy abolished March 21, 1975.

Ethiopia (*continued*)

Capital: Addis–Ababa 9N01 38E43

1890   Each province used the Local Mean Time of its capital
1936 5/5 S.T. Meridian 45E00
                No Daylight Saving Time

FAEROE ISLANDS (Faroes)
Danish dependency in North Atlantic
                Capital: Torshaven 62N01 6W45

To 1908	Local Mean Time	1981 3/29 - 9/26	1986 3/30 - 9/28
1908 1/11	Adopted S.T. Meridian 0W00	1982 3/28 - 9/25	1987 3/29 - 9/27
		1983 3/25 - 9/29	1988 3/27 - 9/25
	No Daylight Saving Time	1984 3/21 - 9/28	1989 3/26 - 9/24
		1985 3/22 - 9/27	1990 3/25 - 9/39

FALKLAND ISLANDS AND DEPENDENCIES
British dependency in South Atlantic, including South Georgia and South Sandwich Islands
                Capital: Stanley 51S42 57W50

Falklands
To 1912   Local Mean Time of 57W50
   1912 3/12 S.T. Meridian 60W00

DAYLIGHT SAVING TIME OBSERVED
(All changes at 0 hr)

	1981 - 82 No DST
	1983 9/25 - 1984 4/28
	1984 9/16 - 1985 4/27
1937 9/26 - 1938 3/20	1985 9/29 - 1986 4/26
1938 9/25 - 1939 3/19	1986 9/15 - 1987 4/20
1939 10/1 - 1940 3/24	1987 9/14 - 1988 4/19
1940 9/29 - 1941 3/23	1988 9/13 - 1989 4/17
1941 9/28 - 1942 3/22	1989 9/18 - 1990 4/16
1942 9/27 -1943 1/1	1990 9/17 - 1991 4/15

South Georgia
To 1912   Local Mean Time of 31W45
   1912 3/12 S.T. Meridian 30W00

Sandwich
To 1912   Local Mean Time of 31W45
   1912 3/12 S.T. Meridian 30W00

FANNING ISLAND See Gilbert Islands

FAROES–ISLANDS See Faeroe Islands

FEDERAL REPUBLIC OF CAMEROON See Cameroon

FEDERATED MALAY STATES See Malaya

FEDERATION INDOCHINOISE   See French Indo-China

FERNANDO DE NORONHA   See Brazil

FERNANDO PO   See Equatorial Guinea

FIJI ISLANDS
    British dependency in the South Pacific
                Capital: Suva   18S09   178E26

To 1915   Local Mean Time of Suva   178E26
   1915   10/26   S.T. Meridian   180E00
                    No Daylight Saving Time

FINLAND

Republic in Northern Europe		1981 3/29 - 9/26
		1982 3/28 - 9/25
Capital: Helsinki 60N09 24E58		1983 3/27 - 9/24
		1984 3/28 - 9/23
To 1921	Local Mean Time of Helsinki 24E58	1985 3/31 - 9/28
1921 5/1	Adopted S.T. Meridian 30E00	1986 3/30 - 9/28
	OBSERVED DAYLIGHT SAVING TIME	1987 3/29 - 9/27
	1942 4/3 - 10/3 0 hr	1988 3/27 - 9/25
		1989 3/26 - 9/24
		1990 3/25 - 9/30

FLINDERS ISLAND
    Northeast of Tasmania

    S.T. Meridian   150E00
                   No Daylight Saving Time

FLORES   See Netherlands East Indies

FORMENTERA   See Balearic Islands

FORMOSA   See Taiwan Republic

FRANCE
    Republic in Western Europe
                Capital: Paris 48N50 2E20 (Observatoire)

1582 12/20   24 hour (12/10 OS) Adopted Gregorian calendar
1793 11/24   Adopted Republic Calendar of France
1806 1/1   Reinstated Gregorian calendar
To 1816   Local Mean Time
  1816   Local Mean Time of Paris 2E20. Although legalized, this time was used only
                  by the government, not the people.
  1891 3/15   0:01 am Local Mean Time of Paris 2E20 adopted throughout the country
  1911 3/9   0 hr Adopted S.T. Meridian 0E00 (except Corsica Island which continued
                  on Local Mean Time of 0E35). However, they were so attached to the
                  Parisian meridian, that they took as lawful time the Local Mean Time
                  of Paris.

France (*Continued*)
    1945 9/16   3 am   Adopted S.T. Meridian 15E00

DAYLIGHT SAVING TIME OBSERVED
(Begins 11 pm; ends 0 hr)

1916 6/14 - 10/2	1926 4/17 - 10/3	1935 3/30 - 10/6
1917 3/24 - 10/8	1927 4/9 - 10/2	1936 4/18 - 10/4
1918 3/9 - 10/7	1928 4/14 - 10/7	1937 4/3 - 10/3
1919 3/1 - 10/6	1929 4/20 - 10/6	1938 3/26 - 10/2
1920 2/14 - 10/26	1930 4/12 - 10/5	1939 4/15 - 11/19
1921 3/14 - 10/26	1931 4/18 - 10/4	**1940 2/24 - 1945 9/16**
1922 3/25 - 10/8	1932 4/2 - 10/2	1976 3/28 1 am - 9/26 0 am
1923 5/26 - 10/7	1933 3/25 - 10/8	1977 4/3 1 am - 9/25 1 am
1924 3/29 - 10/5	1934 4/7 - 10/7	1978 4/2 1 am - 10/1 1 am
1925 4/4 - 10/4		1979 4/1 1 am - 9/30 1 am
		1980 4/6 1 am - 9/26 1 am

1981 3/29 - 9/26
1982 3/28 - 9/25
1983 3/25 - 9/29
1984 3/31 - 9/28
1985 3/31 - 9/27
1986 3/30 - 9/28
1987 3/29 - 9/27
1988 3/27 - 9/25
1989 3/26 - 9/24
1990 3/25 - 9/30

Add 1 more hour for DOUBLE SUMMER TIME

Occupied Zone
1940 6/16 - 1942 11/2 (3 am)

Free Zone
1941 5/4 - 10/6
1942 3/8 - 11/2 (3 am)

Both Zones
1943 3/29 2 am - 11/4 3 am
1944 4/3 2 am - 10/8 1 am
1945 4/2 2 am - 9/16 3 am
1946 - 1975 Not observed
1976 3/28 - 9/26
1977 4/3 - 9/24

FRENCH CAMEROONS See **Cameroon**

FRENCH EQUATORIAL AFRICA (French Congo)
Formerly French Crown Colony. Now **Central African Republic** and **Chad** (see both).
            Capital: Brazzaville 4S17 15E14

    1912 1/1 Adopted S.T. Meridian 15E00
                    No Daylight Saving Time

FRENCH ESTABLISHMENTS IN INDIA
French colony in Indian subcontinent, Chandernagor, Kirkal, Mahe, Pondicherry, Yanaon.
They became part of India in 1952–54.
            Pondicherry 11N56 79E50

    1911 7/18   Adopted S.T. Meridian 82E30

FRENCH ESTABLISHMENTS IN OCEANIA   See French Polynesia

FRENCH GUIANA
   French colony in South America. Became French Overseas Department in 1947.
   Capital: Cayene 4N57 52W20

To 1911		Local Mean Time
1911	7/1	Adopted S.T. Meridian 60W00
		No Daylight Saving Time

FRENCH GUINEA   See Guinea

FRENCH INDIA   See French Establishments in India

FRENCH INDO–CHINA
   French colony in Southeast Asia. *Provinces:* Annam, Cambodia, Cochin–China, Laos and Tonkin

   Capital: Saigon, Cochin–China 10N47 106E41

1906	6/9	Local Mean Time of Phu-Lien observatory 106E35
1911	3/11	0:01 am Annam and Cambodia adopted S.T. Meridian 105E00, Laos adopted 105E00, used by government only. Other provinces observed S.T. Meridian 120E00.
1912	5/1	S.T. Meridian 120E00 nation-wide
1931	5/1	S.T. Meridian 105E00 nation-wide
		No Daylight Saving Time

   See also **Cambodia, Laos** and **Vietnam** (formed by Annam, Cochin–China and Tonkin)

FRENCH LEEWARD ISLANDS   See Leeward Islands

FRENCH MOROCCO
   Formerly French Zone in North Africa. Now part of Morocco.
   Capital: Rabat 34N01 6W51

To 1913	Local Mean Time
1913 10/26	S.T. Meridian 0W00

DAYLIGHT SAVING TIME OBSERVED
1939 9/12 0 hr - 11/19 0 hr
1940 2/25 0 hr - 1945 11/18 0 hr Year round
1946 - 1949 Not observed
1950 6/11 0 hr - 10/29 0 hr
1951 - 1966 Not observed
1967 6/3 Noon - 10/1 0 hr
1968 - 1973 Not observed
1974 6/24 0 hr - 9/1 0 hr (Energy crisis)

FRENCH POLYNESIA
French territory in the South Pacific, including five archipelagoes formed by many islands, including Society Islands, Marquesas Islands, Tuamotu Archipelago, Gambier Islands, Austral (Tubuai) Islands, and Rapa Islands
> Capital: Papeete, Tahiti 17S32 149W34

1912 10/1 S.T. Meridian 150W00
> No Daylight Saving Time

FRENCH SOMALILAND
French colony in East Africa. On March 19, 1967, changed name to French Territory of Afars and Issas
> Capital: Djibouti 11N36 43E07

To 1911   Local Mean Time of Djibouti 43E07
  1911 7/1 Adopted S.T. Meridian 45E00
> No Daylight Saving Time

FRENCH TOGOLAND See Togo

FRENCH WEST AFRICA (French Soudan)
Formerly French Colony in Africa.
> Capital: Dakar, Senegal 14N40 17W26

1912 1/1   Adopted S.T. Meridian 0W00
1934 2/26 Provinces assigned to three S.T. Meridians: 0W00, 15W00, 15E00

PROVINCES
French Guinea Became independent October 2, 1958. (See **Guinea**)
1912 1/1   Adopted S.T. Meridian 15W00
1934 2/26 Adopted S.T. Meridian 0W00

Mauritania Became independent November 18, 1060. (See **Mauritania**)
1912 1/1   Adopted S.T. Meridian 0W00
1934 2/26 Adopted S.T. Meridian 15W00
1960   Adopted S.T. Meridian 0W00

Senegal Became independent August 20, 1960. (See **Senegal**)
1912 1/1   Adopted S.T. Meridian 15W00
1941 6/1 0 hr. Adopted S.T. Meridian 0W00

Soudan Became independent September 22, 1960. (See **Mali**)
1912 1/1   Adopted S.T. Meridian 0W00
1934 2/26 Adopted S.T. Meridian 15W00
1960   Adopted S.T. Meridian 0W00

Dahomey Became independent August 1, 1960. (See **Dahomey**)
1912 1/1   Adopted S.T. Meridian 0E00

French West Africa (*continued*)
    Ivory Coast Became independent August 7, 1960. (See **Ivory Coast**)
    1911 1/1   Adopted S.T. Meridian 0E00
    1934 2/26 Adopted S.T. Meridian 15E00

    Western Niger Became independent August 3, 1960. See **Niger**)
    1912 1/1   Adopted S.T. Meridian 0E00

    Eastern Niger Became independent October 1, 1960. See **Niger**)
    1934 2/26 Adopted S.T. Meridian 15E00
                   No Daylight Saving Time

FRENCH WEST INDIES See **Guadeloupe** and **Martinique**

FRIENDLY ISLANDS See **Tonga Islands**

FRIESLAND See **Netherlands**

FUKIEN See **China**

FUNAFUTI ISLAND See **Tuvalu**

FUTUNA ISLAND See **New Caledonia**

GABON
    Formerly part of French Equatorial Africa. Became independent republic August 17, 1960
            Capital: Libreville 0N23 9E26

    1912 1/1   Adopted S.T. Meridian 15E00
                No Daylight Saving Time

GALAPAGOS ISLANDS (Archipelago of Columbus)
    Territory of Ecuador in Pacific Ocean
            Capital: San Cristobal 0S59 89W30

    S.T. Meridian 75W00
              No Daylight Saving Time

GALICIA PROVINCE See **Poland** or **Spain**

GAMBIA
    Located in West Africa. Formerly French Africa and British colony and protectorate. Became independent February 18, 1965.
            Capital: Banjul 13N28 16W39

    1912 1/1   Adopted S.T. Meridian 15W00
    1918   Adopted S.T. Meridian 0W00
    1933 4/1   Adopted S.T. Meridian 15W00

Gambia (*continued*)
    1963   Adopted S.T. Meridian 0W00
                            No Daylight Saving Time

GAMBIER ISLANDS See French Polynesia

GEORGIAN S.S.R. See Soviet Union

GERMAN EAST AFRICA See Belgian Congo and Tanganyika

GERMAN NEW GUINEA See New Guinea

GERMAN POLAND See Poland

GERMAN SAMOA See Western Samoa

GERMAN SOLOMON ISLANDS See New Guinea

GERMANY
    Formerly republic in Europe. now divided
                    Capital: Berlin 52N30 13E23

    1583 10/16 (NS) Bavaria adopted Gregorian Calendar
    1583 11/14 (NS) Catholics adopted Gregorian Calendar
    1682 3/1   (NS) Strassburg adopted Gregorian Calendar
    1699 11/15 (NS) Protestants adopted Gregorian Calendar
    1700 12/12 (NS) Utrecht adopted Gregorian Calendar
    To 1890   Local Mean Time
        1890 7/30 Railroads began observing S.T. Meridian 15E00
        1891 3/15
    to 1892 3/31 Baden: Local Mean Time of Karlsruhe 8E24
                    Bavaria: Local Mean Time of Munich 11E33
                    Rheinland-Pfalz: Local Mean Time of Ludwigshafen 8E26
                    Wuerttemberg: Local Mean Time of Stuttgart 9E11
        1891 6/1   Prussian railroads observing S.T. Meridian 15E00
        1892 4/1   Southern Germany observing S.T. Meridian 15E00 (Southern Germany
                    included the four kingdoms and dukedoms listed above under 1891 3/15)
        1893 4/1   All of Germany and Prussia observing S.T. Meridian 15E00

                    DAYLIGHT SAVING TIME OBSERVED
                    1916 4/30 11 pm - 1916 10/1 1 am
                    1917 4/16 2 am - 1917 9/17 3 am
                    1918 4/15 2 am - 1918 9/16 3 am
                    1919 - 1939 Not observed nation-wide
        1919 1/1 11 pm GMT French-occupied Rhine bridgeheads shifted to S.T. Meridian
                    0E00. These territories included Mainz, Koblenz, Cologne, Wiesbaden,
                    Mannheim and their areas*, which observed Daylight Savings Time
    *Check with local authorities.

Germany (*continued*)

as follows (begins 11 pm; ends 0 hr):

1919 3/1 - 10/6	1923 5/26 - 10/7
1920 2/14 - 10/26	1924 3/29 - 10/5
1921 3/14 - 10/26	1925 4/4 - 10/4
1922 3/25 - 10/8	1926 4/17 - 10/3

1927 4/9 - 11 pm Returned to S.T. Meridian of 15E00

1940 4/1 2 am - 1942 11/2 3 am

1943 3/29 2 am - 1943 10/4 3 am

1944 4/3 2 am - 1944 10/2 3 am (not 10/8 0h)

1945 4/2 2 am - 1945 9/16 2 am (West Zone)

1945 4/2 2 am - 1945 11/18 2 am (East Zone)

NOTE: German Double Summer Time from 5/24/45 to 9/23/45:

a) When Summer Time ended in the West Zone (West Germany) on 9/16/45, Berlin observed Moscow Time—working time in businesses, shops, factories, theaters, etc.

b) In Berlin and the Soviet-occupied areas:
First, the few trains operating went by Moscow Time (e.g., German Double Summer Time). Authorized travelers reported that some cities adopted railroad time (German Double Summer Time); other cities adopted Standard Time of 15E00, and some cities used ordinary German Summer Time. For this reason, German Double Summer Time must be considered unstable.*

In Leipzig the people used the ordinary German Summer Time. When Leipzig was evacuated by the U.S. troops on 7/3/45 in exchange for West Berlin, the Soviet troops moved in. They introduced Moscow Time for the railroad only. The railroad clock was advanced 1 hour.

In the smaller cities in Saxonia, all the people adopted the time of the railroad clock, which showed German Double Summer Time.

c) Situation went back to normal only after 11/18/45.

1946 4/14 2 am - 1946 10/7 3 am

East Zone

1947 5/11 3 am - 1947 6/29 3 am[†]

1948 4/18 3 am - 1948 10/3 3 am

1949 4/10 3 am - 1949 10/2 3 am

*Check with local authorities

† Double Summer Time (add 1 more hour)

Germany (*continued*)

West Zone
1947 4/6 2 am - 1947 10/5 3 am
1948 4/18 2 am - 1948 10/3 3 am
1949 4/10 2 am - 1949 10/2 3 am
1950 on — See **Germany, East** and **Germany, West**

GERMANY, EAST (see **Germany**)
German Democratic Republic formed October 7, 1949
Capital: East Berlin 52N30 13E25

S.T. Meridian 15E00

Germany, East		
1981 3/29 - 9/26	1986 3/30 - 9/28	
1982 3/28 - 9/25	1987 3/29 - 9/27	
1983 3/25 - 9/29	1988 3/27 - 9/25	
1984 3/31e - 9/28e	1989 3/26 - 9/24	
1985 3/31e - 9/27e	1990 3/25 - 9/30	

GERMANY, WEST (see **Germany**)
Federal Republic formed **May 23, 1949**
Capital: Bonn 50N44 7E05

S.T. Meridian 15E00

DAYLIGHT SAVING TIME OBSERVED
1980 4/6 2 am – 9/28 3 am

Germany, West	(Begins 2 AM, ends 3 AM)
1981 3/29 - 9/26	1986 3/31 - 9/28
1982 3/28 - 9/25	1987 3/29 - 9/27
1983 3/25 - 9/29	1988 3/27 - 9/25
1984 3/31 - 9/28	1989 3/26 - 9/24
1985 3/31 - 9/27	1990 3/25 - 9/30

GHANA
Former British colonies Ashanti, British Togoland, Gold Coast and Northern Territory.
Became independent March 6, 1957, and a republic July 1, 1960.
Capital: Accra 5N31 0W14

S.T. Meridian 0W00

No Daylight Saving Time

GIBRALTAR
British colony, peninsula in Western Mediterranean
Capital: Gibraltar 36N09 5W21

S.T. Meridian 0W00

1981 No DST	1986 3/30 - 9/28
1982 3/28 - 9/25	1987 3/29 - 9/27
1983 3/25 - 9/29	1988 3/27 - 9/25
1984 3/31e - 9/28e	1989 3/26 - 9/24
1985 3/31 - 9/27	1990 3/25 - 9/30

Daylight Saving Time same as **Great Britain**

GILBERT ISLANDS
A group of islands in the South Pacific straddling the international dateline. Some are U.S. possessions or claimed by the U.S.; viz. Baker, Canton, Christmas, Enderbury, Howland, Hull (Orona). Dependency granted self-government in 1971
Capital: Bairiki 1N20 173E01
Administrative Center: Tabiang, Ocean Island 0S53 169E35

S.T. Meridian 160W00 — Christmas, Fanning, Line and Washington Islands
S.T. Meridian 180W00 — Baker, Canton, Enderbury, Gardner (Nikumaroro), Howland, Hull (Orono), Phoenix, and Sydney (Manra) Islands
S.T. Meridian 170E00 — Gilbert, Ocean and Tarawa Islands
No Daylight Saving Time

GOA See **Portuguese India**

GOLD COAST COLONY (West Africa)
With Ashanti and Northern territories, and Togoland. Formerly British colony. Now independent as Ghana, Togo, etc.
Capital: Accra 5N31 0W14

1918(?) Adopted S.T. Meridian 0W00

DAYLIGHT SAVING TIME OBSERVED
(20 minutes advance only)

1918 - 1935 Not observed
1936 9/1 - 1936 12/31
1937 9/1 - 1937 12/31
1938 9/1 - 1938 12/31
1939 9/1 - 1939 12/31
1940 9/1 - 1940 12/31
1941 9/1 - 1941 12/31
1942 9/1 - 1942 12/31
1943 - 1970 Not observed

GRANDE BRETAGNE See Great Britain

GREAT BRITAIN
Kingdom west of Europe
Capital: London 51N31 0W06 (St. Paul's Cathedral)

Includes: Scotland (capital, Edinburgh 55N57 3W11)
Northern Ireland (capital, Belfast 54N36 5W55)
Channel Islands 49N35 2W30
Isle of Man 54N10 4W40
Wales 52N30 3W30

1752 9/14 (NS) Adopted Gregorian calendar
To   1880   Local Mean Time
    1880 1/1 Adopted S.T. Meridian 0W00 (except Scotland and Ireland)
    1884 1/29 Scotland adopted S.T. Meridian 0W00
    1968 2/18 2 am Adopted S.T. Meridian 15E00 (including Northern Ireland)
    1971 11/1 0 hr Reverted to S.T. Meridian 0W00 (including Northern Ireland)

Northern Ireland (Ulster)
    1880 1/1 Local Mean Time of Belfast 5W55
    1916 10/1 Adopted S.T. Meridian 0W00
    1916 5/21
to 1945 7/24 2 am Observed Daylight Saving Time continuously, including winters. However, in several parts of rural Ireland, Daylight Saving Time was never observed. Some remote places observed Local Mean Time. These should be checked with local authorities.
    1945 on   Daylight Saving Time same as England

Great Britain (*continued*)

DAYLIGHT SAVING TIME OBSERVED
(Changes at 2 am except ending dates of Double Summer Time*)

1916 - 1920   England and Scotland observed Daylight Saving Time only on dates below
1921 and after   Also observed as below by Northern Ireland (see note above), Channel Islands, Isle of Man, and Wales

1916 5/21 - 10/1	1948 4/18 - 10/31	(Changes at 1 AM)
1917 4/8 - 9/17	1949 4/3 - 10/30	1981 3/22 - 10/25
1918 3/24 - 9/30	1950 4/16 - 10/22	1982 3/28 - 10/24
1919 3/30 - 9/29	1951 4/15 - 10/21	1983 3/27 - 10/23
1920 3/28 - 10/25	1952 4/20 - 10/26	1984 3/25 - 10/28
1921 4/3 - 10/3	1953 4/19 - 10/4	1985 3/21 - 10/27
1922 3/26 - 10/8	1954 4/11 - 10/3	1986 3/30 - 10/26
1923 4/22 - 9/16	1955 4/17 - 10/2	1987 3/29 - 10/25
1924 4/13 - 9/21	1956 4/22 - 10/7	1988 3/27 - 10/30
1925 4/19 - 10/4	1957 4/14 - 10/6	1989 3/26 - 10/29
1926 4/18 - 10/3	1958 4/20 - 10/5	1990 3/25 - 10/28
1927 4/10 - 10/2	1959 4/19 - 10/4	
1928 4/22 - 10/7	1960 4/10 - 10/2	
1929 4/25 - 10/6	1961 3/26 - 10/29	
1930 4/13 - 10/5	1962 3/25 - 10/28	
1931 4/19 - 10/4	1963 3/31 - 10/27	
1932 4/17 - 10/2	1964 3/22 - 10/25	
1933 4/9 - 10/8	1965 3/21 - 10/24	
1934 4/22 - 10/7	1966 3/20 - 10/23	
1935 4/14 - 10/6	1967 3/19 - 10/29	
1936 4/19 - 10/4	1968 2/18 - 1971 10/31	
1937 4/4 - 10/3	1972 3/19 - 10/29	
1938 4/10 - 10/2	1973 3/18 - 10/28	
1939 4/10 - 11/19	1974 3/17 - 10/27	
1940 2/25 - 12/31	1975 3/16 - 10/26	
*1941 1/1 0 hr	1976 3/21 - 10/24	
through	1977 3/20 - 10/23	
1945 12/31	1978 3/19 - 10/29	
1946 1/1 - 10/6	1979 3/18 - 10/28	
*1947 3/16 - 11/2	1980 3/16 - 10/26	

*Add 1 more hour for DOUBLE SUMMER TIME
(Changes 3 am)

1941 5/4 - 8/10	1945 4/2 - 7/15
1942 4/5 - 8/9	1946 Not observed
1943 4/4 - 8/15	1947 4/13 - 8/10
1944 4/2 - 9/17	

GREECE
Kingdom in Southeastern Europe
Capital: Athens 37N59 23E43

Greece (*continued*)

1846 to 1916 Old Style Calender (Julian) used. (To convert dates, see table in *Time Changes in U.S.A.*)

1916 7/15 (OS) Became July 28 (NS). However, the Gregorian calendar was not adopted by the Greek Church until September 30, 1923 (OS); was followed by October 14, 1923 (NS).

1895 9/14   Local Mean Time of Athens 23E43

1916 7/28 0:01 am   Adopted S.T. Meridian 30E00

DAYLIGHT SAVING TIME OBSERVED
(Changes at 0 hr)

1932 7/1 - 9/2	1952 7/1 - 11/2	1986 3/30 - 9/28
1933 - 1940 Not observed	1978 4/2 - 9/30	1987 3/29 - 9/27
1941 4/7 - 4/30	1979 4/1 - 9/29	1988 3/27 - 9/25
1941 4/30 - 1944 10/8 Same as **Germany**	1980 4/6 - 9/27	1989 3/26 - 9/24
1945 - 1952 Not observed	1981 3/29 - 9/26	1990 3/25 - 9/30
	1982 3/28 - 9/25	
	1983 3/24e - 9/29e	
	1984 3/31e - 9/28e	
	1985 3/31e - 9/27e	

GREENLAND

Danish province in the Arctic Ocean. Most habitation is on the coast, as inland is sheathed with ice.

Capital: Godthaab 64N11 51W43

Second Governor's seat: Godhavn 69N15 53W32

1916 7/28   S.T. Meridians 30W00, 45W00, 60W00, 76W00 **assigned**

Angmagssalik 65N40 37W40 — Observes S.T. Meridian 45W00

Etah 78N18 72W39 — Observes S.T. Meridian 60W00

Scoresby Sound 70N30 21W57 — Observes S.T. Meridian 15W00

Thule 76N33 68W50 — Observes S.T. Meridian 60W00

No Daylight Saving Time

1981 - 85 No DST in Thule, Mesters Vig

1981 3/29 - 9/26 in Angmogssalik and West Coast

1982 3/27 - 9/24 in Angmogssalik and West Coast

3/28 - 9/25 Scoresby Sound

1983 3/25 - 9/29

1984 3/31 - 9/28 In 3 places

1985 3/31 - 9/27 above

1986 3/29 - 9/26*

1987 3/28 - 9/25

1988 3/26 - 9/23

1989 3/25 - 9/29

1990 3/31 - 9/28

*except in Thule and Mesters vig

GRENADA

Former British colony in the West Indies, including Carriacou Island and Petit Martinique Island of the Grenadines. Became independent February 7, 1974.

Capital: .Saint George's 12N03 61W45

To 1911   Local Mean Time of Saint George's 61W45

1911 7/1 0 hr S.T. Meridian 60W00

GRENADINES   See Grenada

GROENLANDE   See Greenland

GUADELOUPE AND DEPENDENCIES
French Overseas Department in Lesser Antilles, including part of St. Martin Island, St. Barthelemy Island and Marie-Galante Island

Capital: Basse-Terre 16N00 61W44

To   1911   Local Mean Time
1911 6/8 0 hr Adopted S.T. Meridian 60W00
                No Daylight Saving Time

GUATEMALA
Republic in Central America

Capital: Guatemala City 14N38 90W31

To   1918   Local Mean Time
1918 10/5   Adopted S.T. Meridian 90W00   1981 - 82 No DST
                No Daylight Saving Time until 1973   1983 5/19e - 9/19e
         Observed from 1973 11/25 - 1974 2/24 (changes at 0 hr) 1984 - 85 No DST
                                                     1986 - 90 No DST

GUAYAQUIL   See Ecuador

GUIANA   See British Guiana, French Guiana, Guyana and Surinam

GUINEA
West African republic, formerly French Guinea. Became independent October 2, 1958

Capital: Conakry 9N30 13W43

Was French Guinea:
1912 1/1   Adopted S.T. Meridian 0W00
1934 2/26   Adopted S.T. Meridian 15W00
1960   Returned to S.T. Meridian 0W00
                No Daylight Saving Time

GUINEA-BISSAU
Former colonial possession of Portugal in West Africa. Became independent September 10, 1974.

Capital: Bissau 11N51 15W35

1911 5/26   S.T. Meridian 15W00

GUINEE ESPAGNOLE   See Equatorial Guinea

GUINEE FRANCAISE   See Guinea

GUINEE PORTUGAISE   See Portuguese West Africa

GUYANA
Former British colony in South America. See British Guiana. Became independent May 26, 1966, and a republic in 1970.

Guyana (*continued*)

Capital: Georgetown 6N48 58W10

1915 3/1 Adopted S.T. Meridian 56W15
No Daylight Saving Time

GUYANNE BRITANNIQUE See British Guiana

GUYANNE FRANCAISE See French Guiana

GUYANNE HOLLANDAISE See Surinam

HAITI
Republic in Greater Antilles
Capital: Port-au-Prince 18N33 72W20

To 1917 Local Mean Time of Port-au-Prince 72W20
1917 1/24 Noon Adopted S.T. Meridian 75W00
No Daylight Saving Time

1981 - 82	No DST
1983	4/29e - 10/27e
1984	4/28e - 10/26e
1985	4/26 - 10/24
1986	4/27 - 10/26
1987	4/26 - 10/25
1988	4/3 - 10/30
1989	4/2 - 10/29
1990	4/1 - 10/28

HACHEMITE, ROYAUME See Jordan

HAINAN ISLAND See China

HAUTE VOLTA See Upper Volta

HEBRIDES ISLANDS See Great Britain

HEDJOZ, HOJOZ See Saudi Arabia

HEILUNGKIANG See China

HERZEGOVINA See Yugoslavia

HINDUSTAN See India

HOKKAIDO See Japan

HOLLAND See Netherlands

HOLLANDIA ISLAND See Netherlands East Indies

HONAN See China

HONDURAS
Republic in Central America
Capital: Tegucigalpa 14N06 87W13

DST

Honduras (continued)
S.T. Meridian 90W00

1981 10/1 - 1982 2/13	1986 10/1 - 1987 2/13
1982 10/1 - 1983 2/12	1987 10/1 - 1988 2/12
1983 10/1 - 1984 2/11	1988 10/1 - 1989 2/10
1984 10/1 - 1985 2/9	1989 10/1 - 1990 2/9
1985 10/1 - 1986 2/8	1990 10/1 - 1991 2/13

No Daylight Saving Time

HONDURAS BRITANNIQUE See British Honduras

HONG KONG
British colony in South China Sea
Capital: Victoria 22N17 114E09

1904 10/30 S.T. Meridian 120E00

DAYLIGHT SAVING TIME OBSERVED
(Changes at 3:30 am)

1946 4/20 - 12/1	1962 3/18 - 11/4
1947 4/13 - 12/30	1963 3/24 - 11/3
1948 5/2 - 10/31	1964 3/22 - 11/1
1949 4/3 - 10/30	1965 4/18 - 10/17
1950 4/2 - 10/29	1966 4/17 - 10/16
1951 4/1 - 10/28	1967 4/16 - 10/22
1952 4/6 - 10/25	1968 4/21 - 10/20
1953 4/5 - 11/1	1969 4/20 - 10/19
1954 3/21 - 10/31	1970 4/19 - 10/18
1955 3/20 - 11/6	1971 4/18 - 10/17
1956 3/18 - 11/4	1972 4/16 - 10/22
1957 3/24 - 11/3	1973 4/22 - 10/21
1958 3/23 - 11/2	1973 12/30 - 1974 10/20*
1959 3/22 - 11/1	1975 4/20 - 10/19
1960 3/20 - 11/6	1976 4/18 - 10/17
1961 3/19 - 11/5	1977 4/17 - 10/16
	1980 5/11 - 10/19

*Period extended due to fuel shortage

See also **China**

HONGRIE See Hungary

HONSHU See Japan

HOORN or **HORN ISLANDS** See New Caledonia and Dependencies

HOPEI See China

HOWLAND ISLAND See Gilbert Islands

HUNAN See China

HUNGARY

Located in Central Europe. Former kingdom, now communist state: Hungarian People's Republic.

Capital: Budapest 47N30 19E05

1587	11/1	Adopted Gregorian Calendar
To	1890	Local Mean Time
1890	10/1	Adopted S.T. Meridian 15E00

DAYLIGHT SAVING TIME OBSERVED

1916 4/30 11 pm - 1916 10/1 1 am	1941 4/6 2 am - 1945 9/16 (continuously)
1917 4/16 3 am - 1917 9/17 3 am	1980 3/31 - 9/30
1918 - 1940 Not observed	

1981 3/29 - 9/26	1986 3/30 - 9/28
1982 3/28 - 9/25	1987 3/29 - 9/27
1983 3/25e - 9/29e	1988 3/27 - 9/25
1984 3/31e - 9/28e	1989 3/26 - 9/24
1985 3/31 - 9/27	1990 3/25 - 9/30

HUON ISLANDS See New Caledonia

IADRONE ISLANDS See South Sea Mandated Territories

IBIZA ISLAND See Balearic Islands

ICELAND

Former sovereign state in union with Denmark. Became an independent republic June 17, 1944

Capital: Reykjavik 64N09 21W57

1837	1/1	Local Mean Time of Reykjavik 21W57
1908	1/1	Adopted S.T. Meridian 15W00

DAYLIGHT SAVING TIME OBSERVED

1917 2/20 - 10/25	1966 4/3 - 10/23
1918 2/20 - 11/15	1967 4/2 - 10/22
1919 2/19 - 11/15	1968 4/7 - 10/27
1920 - 1940 Not observed	1969 4/6 - 10/26
1941 3/1 - 7/?	1970 4/5 - 10/25
1942 3/7 - 7/?	1971 4/4 - 10/31
1943 - 1960 Unconfirmed	1972 4/2 - 10/29
1960 4/3 - 10/30	1973 4/1 - 10/28
1961 4/2 - 10/29	1974 4/7 - 10/27
1962 4/1 - 10/28	1975 4/6 - 10/26
1963 4/7 - 10/27	1976 4/4 - 10/31
1964 4/5 - 10/25	1977 4/3 - 10/30
1965 4/4 - 10/31	1980 3/31 - 9/30
	1981 - 85 No DST
	1986 - 90 No DST

IFNI

Former Spanish colony in West Africa. On June 30, 1969, became part of Morocco.

Capital: Sidi Ifni 29N23 10W10

S.T. Meridian 0W00

ILE DE L'ASCENCION See **Ascension Island**

ILE DU PRINCE See **Portuguese West Africa**

ILES DU CAP-VERT See **Cape Verde Islands**

INDE BRITANNIQUE See **India**

INDE HOLLANDAISE See **Netherlands Antilles** and **Netherlands East Indies**

INDE PORTUGAISE See **Portuguese India**

INDIA

Former empire under British rule. Became independent August 15, 1947, and a democratic republic January 26, 1950

> Capital: New Delhi 28N38 77E13

1947	8/15	Country divided into two nations: Hindustan and Pakistan (see **Pakistan**)
To	1906	Local Mean Time of Madras 80E15 was legal time
1907	1/1	Adopted S.T. Meridian 82E30. Used by government but many cities remained on Local Mean Time.
1911	7/18	French Establishments and Portuguese Goa adopted S.T. Meridian 82E30
1920		Burma, in Bengal province, adopted S.T. Meridian 97E30
1941	1/10	Calcutta, which had always observed Local Mean Time 88E20, adopted S.T. Meridian 97E30
1947	8/15	Hindustan (India) on S.T. Meridian 82E30

DAYLIGHT SAVING TIME OBSERVED
1942 9/1 - 1945 10/15 except:

Bengal Province
1941 10/1 - 1942 5/15
1942 9/1 - 1947 10/14

Assam Province
1941 11/1 - 1942 5/15
1942 9/1 - 1945 10/15

Bihar Province
1941 12/1 - 1942 5/15
1942 9/1 - 1945 10/15

INDO-CHINA See **French Indo-China**

INDO-CHINESE FEDERATION See **French Indo-China**

INDONESIA

World's largest archipelago comprised of about 13,000 islands, located between the Indian Ocean and the Pacific Ocean. Formerly Netherlands East Indies. Became independent

Indonesia (*continued*)
December 28, 1949. Name formally changed to Republic of Indonesia on August 15, 1950.
On July 17, 1976 Portuguese Timor became Indonesia's 27th province. Some of the others
are Java, Sumatra, Kalimantan, Celebes, West Irian, Bangka, Billiton, Madura, Bali.
Capital: Jakarta, Java 6S10 106E48

For time zones see Netherlands East Indies
No Daylight Saving Time

INNER MONGOLIA   See China

IRAN
Kingdom in Western Asia
Capital: Tehran 35N40 51E26

1916		Adopted Local Mean Time of Teheran 51E26
1926		S.T. Meridian 52E30
1976	3/14	Adopted Monarchic Calendar. (Add 1,180 years to Iranian Solar Calendar, or 559 years to current Gregorian Calendar.) Muslim Lunar Calendar, used for religious holidays, not affected. Within five years all government documents will be changed to reflect Monarchic dates.
1977		S.T. Meridian 60E00

DAYLIGHT SAVING TIME OBSERVED
Add ½ hr.

1978 3/23 - 9/20   1979 3/21 - 9/19   1980 3/23 - 9/21

(Add ½ hour)
1981 3/29 - 9/27
1982 3/28 - 9/26
1983 3/27 - 9/25
1984 3/25 - 9/23
1985 3/31 - 9/29
1986 - 90 DST not observed country-wide.
Check with local authorities.

IRAQ (Mesopotamia)
Kingdom in Western Asia
Capital: Baghdad 33N20 44E24

Arabic time, based on setting of sun, used by mass Moslem population.

1890s		Little by little the Local Mean Time of Baghdad 44E24 was imposed country-wide
1918	1/1	S.T. Meridian 45E00

No Daylight Saving Time

1981 - 82 No DST
1983 3/31e - 9/30e
1984 4/1 - 9/29
1985 ?
1986 - 90 DST not standardized country-wide.
Check with local authorities.

IRELAND   See Great Britain and Eire

IRIAN   See Netherlands East Indies

IRISH FREE STATE   See Eire

ISLAND   See Iceland

ISLAS MALVINAS   See Falkland Islands

ISLE OF CLOVES   See Zanzibar

ISLE OF MAN   See Great Britain

ISLE OF PINES   See New Caledonia

ISRAEL

Former British mandated territory called Palestine. Became independent May 14, 1948.

Capital: Jerusalem 31N47 35E10

Diplomatic Capital: Tel Aviv 32N04 34E46

S.T. Meridian 30E00

See **Palestine** for time information before 1948

DAYLIGHT SAVING TIME OBSERVED

*1948 5/23 0 hr - 9/1 0 hr	1955 6/11 2 am - 9/11 0 hr	1981 - 83 No DST
1948 9/1 0 hr - 11/1 2 am	1956 6/3 0 hr - 9/30 3 am	1984 5/5e - 8/31e
1949 5/1 0 hr - 11/1 2 am	1957 4/29 2 am - 9/22 0 hr	1985 - ?
1950 4/16 0 hr - 9/15 3 am	1958 - 1973 Not observed	1986 5/17 - 9/6
1951 4/1 0 hr - 11/11 3 am	1974 7/7 0 hr - 10/13 0 hr	1987 4/15 - 9/13
1952 4/20 2 am - 10/19 3 am	1975 4/20 0 hr - 8/31 0 hr	1988 4/15 - 9/13
1953 4/12 2 am - 9/13 3 am	1976-1977 Not observed	1989 4/13 - 9/11
1954 6/13 0 hr - 9/12 0 hr		1990 4/12 - 9/17

*Double Summer Time

ITALIAN EAST AFRICA   See **Ethiopia, Eritrea, Italian Somaliland**

ITALIAN SOMALILAND

Italian colony in East Africa

Capital: Mogadiscio 2N02 45E21

1893   11/1   Adopted S.T. Meridian 45E00

No Daylight Saving Time

See also **Somalia**

ITALY

Republic in Southern Europe

Capital: Rome 41N54 12E29

1582	10/15 (NS)	Adopted Gregorian calendar
1866	9/22	Local Mean Time mostly used by railways and telegraph, as follows:
		Italian Peninsula: Local Mean Time of Rome 12E29
		Sardinia: Local Mean Time of Cagiliari 9E06
		Sicily: Local Mean Time of Palermo 13E22
1893	11/1 0 hr	Adopted S.T. Meridian 15E00

DAYLIGHT SAVING TIME OBSERVED

1916 6/4 0 hr - 10/1 0 hr	1943 3/29 2 am - 10/4 3 am
1917 4/1 0 hr - 10/1 0 hr	*1944 4/3 2 am - 10/2 3 am
1918 3/10 0 hr - 10/7 0 hr	1945 4/2 2 am - 9/17 0 hr
1919 3/2 0 hr - 10/5 0 hr	1946 3/17 2 am - 10/6 3 am
1920 3/21 0 hr - 9/19 0 hr	1947 3/16 0 hr - 10/5 1 am
1921 - 1939 Not observed	1948 2/29 2 am - 10/3 3 am
1940 6/15 0 hr - 1942 11/2 3 am	1949 - 1965 Not observed

*North Italy only (Italian Social Republic).

Italy (*continued*)

DST Observed (*continued*)

(Begins 2 AM, ends 3 AM)

1966 5/22 0 hr - 9/25 0 hr	1974 5/26 0 hr - 9/29 0 hr	1981 3/29 - 9/26
1967 5/28 0 hr - 9/24 0 hr	1975 6/1 0 hr - 9/28 0.01 am	1982 3/28 - 9/25
1968 5/26 0 hr - 9/22 0 hr	1976 5/30 0 hr - 9/26 0:01 am	1983 3/25 - 9/29
1969 6/1 0 hr - 9/28 0 hr	1977 5/22 0 hr - 9/25 0:01 am	1984 3/31 - 9/28
1970 5/31 0 hr - 9/27 0 hr	1978 5/28 0 hr - 10/1 0:01 am	1985 3/31 - 9/27
1971 5/23 0 hr - 9/26 0.01 am	1979 5/27 0 hr - 9/10 0:01 am	1986 3/30 - 9/28
1972 5/28 0 hr - 10/1 0 hr	1980 4/6 2 am - 9/28 3 am	1987 3/29 - 9/27
1973 6/3 0 hr - 9/29 0 hr		1988 3/27 - 9/25
		1989 3/26 - 9/24
		1990 3/25 - 9/30

IVORY COAST

Former province of French West Africa. Became independent August 7, 1960
Capital: Abidjan 5N19 4W01

1911 1/1	Adopted S.T. Meridian 0W00	
1934 2/26	Adopted S.T. Meridian 15W00	

No Daylight Saving Time

JAMAICA (Jamaique)

Former British colony in Greater Antilles, with Cayman, Turks and Caicos Islands. Became independent August 6, 1962
Capital: Kingston 18N00 76W48

To 1912	Local Mean Time of Kingston 76W48	
1912 2/1	Adopted S.T. Meridian 75W00	

DAYLIGHT SAVING TIME OBSERVED

1978 4/30 - 10/28	1979 4/29 - 10/27	1980 4/27 - 10/25

1981 4/26 - 10/24	1986 4/27 - 10/26
1982 4/25 - 10/23	1987 4/26 - 10/25
1983 4/29 - 10/26	1988 4/24 - 10/30
1984 4/28 - 10/25	1989 4/30 - 10/27
1985 4/28 - 10/26	1990 4/29 - 10/28

JAN MAYEN

Norwegian island in the Greenland Sea

S.T. Meridian 15E00

JAPAN

Empire off Asia in North Pacific. This island nation consists of 4 main islands and others including Bonin, Daito, Karafuto, Kuril, Marcus, Ryukyu (Okinawa), Volcano (Iwo Jima)
Capital: Tokyo 35N40 139E45

Main Islands	City	Latitude	Longitude
Honshu	Tokyo	35N40	139E45
Hokkaido	Sapporo	43N03	141E19
Kyushu	Nagasaki	32N43	129E52
Shikoku	Kochi	33N32	133E31

1873 1/1 (NS) Adopted Gregorian calendar. (Lunar calendar rescinded — its date was the 5th of Meiji.) However, the populace continued to use the lunar calendar.

Japan (*continued*)

1889 1/1	Adopted S.T. Meridian 135E00. Used by government only, not by civil population.
1896 1/1	Population forced to use S.T. Meridian 135E00. Except Formosa, the Pescadores, Yaeyama and Miyako groups on S.T. Meridian 120E00

DAYLIGHT SAVING TIME OBSERVED *

1948 5/2 1 am - 9/12 0 hour	1981 - 85 No DST
1949 4/3 1 am - 9/11 0 hour	1986 - 90 No DST
1950 5/7 1 am - 9/10 0 hour	
1951 5/6 1 am - 9/09 0 hour	

* The people worked by DST, but births were recorded in Standard Time.

JAPPEN GROUP See Netherlands East Indies

JARVIS ISLAND
British possession, also claimed by U.S. Located in South Pacific.
Radio towers: 0S22 160W02

S.T. Meridian 165W00

JAVA See Netherlands East Indies

JEBEL DRUZ See Levant States

JEMBONGAN ISLAND See Malaysia

JOHORE See Malaya

JORDAN
Former British mandate called Transjordan. Located in Western Asia. Became independent May 25, 1946. Changed name to Hachemite Kingdom of Jordan on April 26, 1949.
Capital: Amman 31N57 35E56

		1986 4/4 - 10/3
		1987 4/3 - 10/2
Until 1920s	Probably used Local Mean Time (unconfirmed)	1988 4/2 - 10/7
1931	Using S.T. Meridian 30E00	1989 4/7 - 10/6
1960 - 1970	On S.T. Meridian 30E00	1990 4/6 - 10/5

DAYLIGHT SAVING TIME OBSERVED
1978 4/30 - 9/30
1981 - 85 No DST

JUDEA See Palestine

JUTLAND See Denmark

KALIMANTAN See Netherlands East Indies

KAMARAN ISLAND (See also Yemen, People's Democratic Republic)
South Yemen islands in the Red Sea

S.T. Meridian 45E00   No Daylight Saving Time

KAMCHATKA See Soviet Union

KANSU See China

KARAFUTO See Japan

KARA KALPAK AREA See Soviet Union

KAZAKH S.S.R. See Soviet Union

KEDAH See Malaya

KEI ISLAND See Netherlands East Indies

KELANTAN See Malaya

KENYA
Former British colony in East Africa. Became a republic December 12, 1963
Capital: Nairobi 1S17 36E48

To 1928		Local Mean Time
1928 6/31	0 hr	Adopted S.T. Meridian 45E00
1930 1/1	0 hr	Adopted S.T. Meridian 37E30
1940s		Observing S.T. Meridian 41E15
By 1960		Observing S.T. Meridian 45E00
		No Daylight Saving Time

KERGUELEN ISLANDS
Madagascar dependency in Indian Ocean
Capital: Port Jeanne d'Arc 49S33 69E49

S.T. Meridian 75E00

KERMADEC ISLANDS
New Zealand dependency in South Pacific
Denham, Flagstaff 29S16 177E57

S.T. Meridian 172E30
1945 11/24 Adopted S.T. Meridian 180E00
No Daylight Saving Time

KHMER REPUBLIC See Cambodia

KIANGSI See China

KIANGSU See China

KINSHASA See Congo (Kinshasa)

KIRGHIZ S.S.R. See Soviet Union

KIRIBATI, REPUBLIC OF 33 Micronesian islands in the mid-Pacific. See the Gilbert, Line and Phoenix groups.

KIRIN See China

KIRKAL See **French Establishments in India**

KOLA PENINSULA See **Soviet Union**

KOREA

Former Japanese territory in Eastern Asia. Now split — after 1948, see **Korea, North** and **Korea, South**   Capital: Seoul   37N32   126E57

To 1904   S.T. Meridian   127E30
1904 12/1 S.T. Meridian   135E00
1928   S.T. Meridian   127E30
1932   S.T. Meridian   135E30
People in country districts used sun dials.

KOREA, NORTH

Former Japanese territory in Eastern Asia. Became communist state May 1, 1948.
Capital: Pyongyang   39N00   126E45

S.T. Meridian   135E00
For time information before 1948, see **Korea**

KOREA, SOUTH

Former Japanese territory in Eastern Asia. Became Korea Democratic People's Republic August 15, 1948.
Capital: Seoul   37N32   126E57

S.T. Meridian   135E00

1954 3/21 Clocks turned back 1 hour until:
1961 8/10 Clocks advanced 30 minutes at 0:01 am to S.T. Meridian 135E00
For time information before 1948, see **Korea**.

DAYLIGHT SAVING TIME OBSERVED
1960 5/? - 9/13   1981 - 85 No DST
1961 - 1971 Not observed   1986 - 90 No DST

KURIL or KURILI ISLANDS

To 1904   Local Mean Time
1904 12/1 S.T. Meridian   135E00
No Daylight Saving Time

KURO ISLAND See **Japan**

KUWAIT

Former British territory. Became independent state of Saudi Arabia on the Arabian Peninsula June 19, 1961
Capital: Kuwait   29N23   47E59

Arabic time, based on setting of sun, has been commonly used.
No Standard or Daylight Saving Time

KWANGSI-CHUANG See **China**

KWANTUNG See China

KWAYALEIN See South Sea Mandated Territories

KWEICHOW See China

KYUSHU See Japan

LABUAN See British North Borneo and Malaya

LACCADIVE ISLANDS See India (Hindustan)

LADRONE ISLANDS See South Sea Mandated Territories

LAO PEOPLE'S DEMOCRATIC REPUBLIC See Laos

LAOS

Formerly part of French Indo-China. Became an independent republic December 3, 1975.
Administrative Capital: Vientiane 17N58 102E37
Royal Capital: Luang Prabang 19N54 102E08

1906 6/9		Local Mean Time of 106E35
1911 3/11	0:01 am	S.T. Meridian 105E00 used by government only
1912 5/1		S.T. Meridian 120E00
1931 5/1		S.T. Meridian 105E00
		No Daylight Saving Time

See also **French Indo-China**

LAS PALMAS See Canary Islands

LATAKIA See Levant States

LATVIA

Former republic in Northern Europe. Now Latvian S.S.R. (See **Soviet Union**).
Capital: Riga 56N55 24E07

To 1918	Local Mean Time of Pulkovo Observatory 30E20
1918 2/15	Adopted Gregorian calendar and Local Mean Time of Riga 24E07
1926 6/11	Adopted S.T. Meridian 30E00

DAYLIGHT SAVING TIME OBSERVED
1918 Dates unconfirmed
1919 4/1 - 5/22
1941 - 1944 Same as Germany

LEBANON

Formerly one of the Levant States in Western Asia. Became independent November 22, 1948.
Capital: Beirut 35N54 35E28

Lebanon (*continued*)
S.T. Meridian 30E00

DAYLIGHT SAVING TIME OBSERVED
(Bierut, during period of British occupation)

1920 3/28 - 10/25	1981 - 83 No DST	1986	5/1 - 10/16
1921 4/3 - 10/3	1984 5/1 - 10/14	1987	5/1 - 10/16
1922 3/26 - 10/8	1985 - ?	1988	5/1 - 10/16
1923 4/22 - 9/16		1989	5/1 - 10/16
1978 4/30 - 9/30		1990	5/1 - 10/16

LEEWARD ISLANDS See Anguilla, Antigua Barbuda, Guadeloupe, Montserrat, Nevis, Redonda, Saba, St. Christopher, St. Eustatius, St. Martin, Sombrero, Virgin Islands

LESOTHO
Former British protectorate (Basutoland) in South Africa. Became independent October 4, 1966, as a kingdom.

Capital: Maseru 29S18 27E30

S.T. Meridian 30E00

No Daylight Saving Time

LETTONIE   See Latvia

LEVANT STATES
Republics in Western Asia
Jebel Druz   Capital: Soueida 32N43 36E34
Latakia   Capital: Latakia 35N31 35E45

S.T. Meridian 30E00

See also **Lebanon** and Syria

LIAONING   See China

LIBERIA
Republic in West Africa

Capital: Monrovia 6N20 10W48

To 1919   Local Mean Time of Monrovia 10W48
1919 3/1   Adopted S.T. Meridian 11W00

No Daylight Saving Time

LIBYA
Former Italian colony in North Africa. Became Arab Republic of Lybia September 1, 1969

Capitals: Tripoli 32N54 13E10
Bengasi 32N06 30E05
Beida (Darnah, Derna) 32N46 22E39

	1981 No DST	1986	4/4 - 10/3
S.T. Meridian 15E00 (Adoption date unknown, probably in 1920s)	1982 4/1 - 9/30	1987	4/4 - 10/2
	1983 4/1e - 9/30e	1988	4/1 - 10/1
	1984 4/1e - 9/30e	1989	4/1 - 10/1
	1985 ?	1990	4/1 - 10/1

LIECHTENSTEIN
Principality located in Central Europe
Capital: Vaduz 47N08 9E31

1894 6/1 S.T. Meridian 15E00
No Daylight Saving Time

1981 - 85	No DST
1986	3/30 - 9/28
1987	3/29 - 9/27
1988	3/27 - 9/25
1989	3/26 - 9/24
1990	3/25 - 9/30

LINGA ARCHIPELAGO See Netherlands East Indies

LITHUANIA
Former republic in Northern Europe. Now Lithuanian S.S.R. (See Soviet Union)
Capital: Kaunas 54N54 23E55

1918 2/15   Adopted Gregorian Calendar

1820 - 1917	Local Mean Time of Warsaw 21E00
1917 - 1919	Local Mean Time of Kaunas 23E55
1919 10/10	S.T. Meridian 15E00
1920 7/12	As part of Russia, S.T. Meridian 30E00
1920 10/9	Occupied by Poland, S.T. Meridian 15E00
1942 - 1944	Same as Germany
1945	S.T. Meridian 30E00

Daylight Saving Time same as Germany 1941-1944

LOMBOK See Netherlands East Indies

LORD HOWE
Islands in the Pacific Ocean off the coast of New South Wales, Australia

S.T. Meridian 150E00
No Daylight Saving Time

LOYALTY ISLANDS See New Caledonia

LUCAVES ISLANDS See Bahamas

LUXEMBOURG
Grand Duchy in Central Europe
Capital: Luxembourg 49N38 6E10

1892 4/1	Adopted S.T. Meridian 15E00
1918 12/1	Adopted S.T. Meridian 0E00
1940 2/24 11 pm	Adopted S.T. Meridian 15E00

DAYLIGHT SAVING TIME OBSERVED
1916 3/1 11 pm - 9/30 10 am	1919 4/15 2 am - 9/15 3 am
1917 4/30 11 pm - 9/30 1 am	1920 2/14 11 pm - 10/23 2 am
1918 4/15 2 am - 9/16 3 am	1921 3/14 11 pm - 10/26 2 am

Luxembourg (*continued*)

1922 3/25 11 pm - 10/8 1 am	1937 4/4 2 am - 10/3 3 am	1981 3/29 - 9/26
1923 4/21 11 pm - 10/7 2 am	1938 3/27 2 am - 10/2 3 am	1982 3/28 - 9/25
1924 3/29 11 pm - 10/5 1 am	1939 4/16 2 am - 11/19 3 am	1983 3/25 - 9/29
1925 4/17 11 pm - 10/4 2 am	1940 5/14 2 am year round	1984 3/31 - 9/28
1926 4/16 11 pm - 10/3 1 am	until 1942 11/1 3 am	1985 3/31 - 9/27
1927 4/9 11 pm - 10/2 1 am	1943 3/29 - 10/3	1986 3/30 - 9/28
1928 4/18 11 pm - 10/7 1 am	1944 4/3 - 9/17	1987 3/28 - 9/27
1929 4/21 11 pm - 10/6 3 am	1945 4/2 - 9/15	1988 3/27 - 9/25
1930 4/13 2 am - 10/5 3 am	1946 5/19 - 10/6	1989 3/26 - 9/24
1931 4/19 2 am - 10/4 3 am	1947 - 1976 Not observed	1990 3/25 - 9/30
1932 4/17 2 am - 10/2 3 am	1977 4/3 - 9/24	
1933 3/26 2 am - 10/8 3 am	1978 4/2 - 9/30	
1934 4/8 2 am - 10/7 3 am	1979 4/1 - 9/29	
1935 3/31 2 am - 10/6 3 am	1980 4/6 - 9/27	
1936 4/19 2 am - 10/4 3 am		

MACAO See Portuguese India

MACEDONIA See Bulgaria, Greece, Yugoslavia

MADAGASCAR (Malagasy)

Former French colony in Indian Ocean near Africa. Became independent republic
June 26, 1960

Capital: Tananarive 18S54 47E30

To 1911   Local Mean Time
1911 7/1   Adopted S.T. Meridian 45E00, but the greater part of the island continues to
use the Local Mean Time of the Tananarive observatory — 47E30.
No Daylight Saving Time

MADEIRA ISLANDS

Portuguese colony in North Atlantic
Capital: Funchal 32N38 16W54

To 1912   Local Mean Time of Funchal 16W54
1912 1/1   Adopted S.T. Meridian 15W00

DAYLIGHT SAVING TIME OBSERVED
(Years prior to 1960 undetermined)

1960 4/3 - 10/2	1967 4/2 - 10/1	1974 4/7 - 10/6
1961 4/2 - 10/1	1968 4/7. - 10/6	1975 4/6 - 10/5
1962 4/1 - 10/7	1969 4/6 - 10/5	1976 4/4 - 10/3
1963 4/7 - 10/6	1970 4/5 - 10/4	1977 4/3 - 10/2
1964 4/5 - 10/4	1971 4/4 - 10/3	1978 4/2 - 10/1
1965 4/4 - 10/3	1972 4/2 - 10/1	1979 4/1 - 10/7
1966 4/3 - 10/2	1973 4/1 - 10/7	1980 4/6 - 10/5

MADURA ISLAND See Netherlands East Indies

MAEHREN See Czechoslovakia

MAHE See French Establishments in India

MAHE ISLAND See Seychelles

MAKASSAR See Netherlands East Indies

MALABAR COAST See India and Portuguese India

MALACCA See Malaya

MALADIVE, ILES See Maldive Islands

MALAGASY REPUBLIC See Madagascar

MALAWALI ISLAND See Malaysia

MALAWI

Former British protectorate (Nyasaland) in East Africa. Became a republic July 6, 1966.
Capital: Lilongwe 13S58 33E45

S.T. Meridian 30E00

No Daylight Saving Time

MALAYA

Former British colonies (British Malaya) located on southern part of Malay Peninsula in
Southeast Asia. Union of Malaya formed in 1946, consisting of Straits Settlements (Malacca,
Penang, Province Wellesley, Dindings, Singapore), the Federated Malay States (Negri Sembilan,
Pahang, Perak, Selangor), the Non-Federated Malay States (Johore, Kedah, Kelantan, Perlis,
Trengganu) and Labuan. In 1948, became Federation of Malaya. On August 31, 1957,
became an independent constitutional monarchy.
Capital: Singapore 1N16 103E51

To 1905   Local Mean Time of Singapore 103E51
   1905 6/1 S.T. Meridian 105E00, except Labuan: S.T. Meridian 120E00 adopted
              1904 10/1
   1933 1/1 0:00:20 am Adopted S.T. Meridian 110E00, except Labuan; remains on
              S.T. Meridian 120E00
By 1960   Using S.T. Meridian 112E30
                         No Daylight Saving Time
See also **Malaysia**

MALAYAN UNION See Malaya

MALAYSIA

The Malay States joined with Singapore, Sabah and Sarawak to form Malaysia on September
16, 1963. In 1965 Singapore separated and became independent. Islands belonging to
Malaysia are Balambangan, Banggi, Jembongan, Malawali.
Capital: Kuala Lumpur 3N10 101E42

Malaysia (*continued*)
  By 1960s S.T. Meridian 112E30, except Sabah and Sarawak: S.T. Meridian 120E00
  1981 12/31 11:30 pm adopted S.T. Meridian 120E00 No Daylight Saving Time
  See also **Malaya**

MALAY STATES See **Malaya**

MALDIVE ISLANDS
  Former British dependency in Indian Ocean. Became a republic November 11, 1968
    Capital: Male 4N10 73E30

  Formerly used Local Mean Time of Male 73E30
  1960s Adopted S.T. Meridian 75E00

MALI
  Former French Soudan in West Africa. Became independent September 22, 1960
    Capital: Bamako 12N39 7W59

  1912 1/1 Adopted S.T. Meridian 0W00
  1934 2/26 Adopted S.T. Meridian 15W00
  1960 Adopted S.T. Meridian 0W00
      No Daylight Saving Time

MALLORCA ISLAND See **Balearic Islands**

MALTA
  Former British colony in the Mediterranean. Became independent September 21, 1964, and a republic on December 13, 1974.
    Capital: Valetta 35N54 14E31

  To 1893 Local Mean Time
  1893 11/2 0 hr S.T. Meridian 15E00

     DAYLIGHT SAVING TIME OBSERVED

1916 6/4 0 hr - 10/1 0 hr	1940 6/15 - 1945 9/30
1917 4/1 0 hr - 10/1 0 hr	1946 - 1977 Not observed
1918 3/10 0 hr - 10/7 0 hr	1978 4/16 - 9/16
1919 3/2 0 hr - 10/5 0 hr	1979 4/15 - 9/15
1920 3/21 0 hr - 9/19 0 hr	1980 4/20 - 9/21
1921 - 1939 Not observed	

1981 3/31 - 9/19	1986 3/30 - 9/28
1982 3/28 - 9/25	1987 3/29 - 9/27
1983 3/25 - 9/29	1988 3/27 - 9/25
1984 3/31e - 9/28e	1989 3/26 - 9/24
1985 3/31 - 9/27	1990 3/15 - 9/30

MALVINAS, MALVINE ISLANDS See **Falkland Islands**

MANCHUKUO See **China (Manchuria)**

MANCHURIA See **China**

MANDATED TERRITORY OF NEW GUINEA See New Guinea

MANDCHOURIE See China

MANGAREVA See Gambia

MANOKWARI See Netherlands East Indies

MARCUS ISLAND See Japan

MARIANA ISLANDS See South Sea Mandated Territories

MARIE-GALANTE ISLAND See Guadeloupe

MAROC See Morocco

MARQUESAS ISLANDS See French Polynesia

MARSHALL ISLANDS See South Sea Mandated Territories

MARTINIQUE
    French department in the West Indies
                Capital: Port de France 14N36 61W05

   To 1911   Local Mean Time of Port de France 61W05
     1911 5/1 Adopted S.T. Meridian 60W00
                  No Daylight Saving Time

MATABELELAND See Rhodesia

MAURITANIA
    Former province of French West Africa. Became an independent Islamic republic
    November 28, 1960
                Capital: Nouakchott 18N06 15W57

   To 1912   Local Mean Time
     1912 1/1   Adopted S.T. Meridian 0W00
     1934 2/26 Adopted S.T. Meridian 15W00
     1960 11/28 Adopted S.T. Meridian 0W00
                  No Daylight Saving Time

MAURITIUS
    Former British colony in Indian Ocean. Became independent March 12, 1968
                Capital: Port Louis 20S09 57E30

   To 1907   Local Mean Time
     1907 1/1   Adopted S.T. Meridian 60E00
                  No Daylight Saving Time

MELILLA See Spain

MENORCA ISLAND See Balearic Islands

MESOPOTAMIA See Iraq

MICRONESIA See South Sea Mandated Territories

MIDDLE CONGO See French Equatorial Africa

MIQUELON ISLAND See Saint Pierre and Miquelon

MIYAKO ISLANDS See Japan

MOLDAVIAN S.S.R. See Soviet Union

MOLUCCAS (Molukken) See Netherlands East Indies

MOLUQUES, ILES See Moluccas

MONACO
>   Principality in Southern Europe
>   Capital: Monaco 43N44 7E26

>   S.T. Meridian 0W00
>   1940 S.T. Meridian 15E00
>   Daylight Saving Time same as **France**

MONGOLIAN PEOPLE'S REPUBLIC
>   A country wedged between Communist China and the Soviet Union
>   Capital: Ulan Bator 47N55 106E45
>   S.T. Meridian 105E00

No DST country wide.
In 1983. 1984, and 1985 DST
observed from 4/1 to 9/30 in
Ulan Bator
Ulan Bator only:
1986 3/30 - 9/28
1987 3/29 - 9/27
1988 3/27 - 9/25
1989 3/26 - 9/30
1990 3/25 - 9/30

MONTENEGRO See Yugoslavia

MONTSERRAT ISLAND
>   British possession in the West Indies
>   Capital: Plymouth 16N42 62W13

>   .To 1911   Local Mean Time
>   1911 7/1 0:01 am S.T. Meridian 60W00
>   No Daylight Saving Time

MORAVIA See Czechoslovakia

MOROCCO
>   Kingdom in North Africa composed of the former French Morocco and Spanish Morocco.
>   Became independent March 2, 1956.

Morocco (*continued*)

Capital: Rabat 34N01 6W51

The Moors used sun time for years.
1917 10/26 Adopted S.T. Meridian 0W00

DAYLIGHT SAVING TIME OBSERVED
1979 6/1 - 7/31   1980 5/1 - 8/1
                          1981 - 85 No DST

DST not observed country-wide.
Check with local authorities.
1986 3/30 - 9/28
1987 3/29 - 9/27
1988 3/27 - 9/25
1989 3/26 - 9/24
1990 3/25 - 9/30

MOROCCO, FRENCH See French Morocco

MOROCCO, SPANISH See Spanish Morocco

MOZAMBIQUE
Republic in Southwest Africa. Formerly part of Portuguese East Africa. Became independent
June 25, 1975.

Capital: Maputo 25S58 32E35

1903 3/1 Adopted S.T. Meridian 30E00
No Daylight Saving Time

MUSCAT AND OMAN See Oman Sultanate

NAMALAND See Union of South Africa

NAMAQUALAND See Union of South Africa

NAMIBIA
Formerly part of the Union of South Africa. The territory is directly administered by the
United Nations.

Capital: Windhoek 22S30 17E00

1903 3/1 S.T. Meridian 30E00
1911   S.T. Meridian 15E00

DAYLIGHT SAVING TIME OBSERVED
(Changes at 2 am)
1942 9/20 - 1943 3/21

NANUMEA ISLAND See Tuvalu

NASHONALAND See Rhodesia

NATAL See Union of South Africa

NAURU
Former British and Australian control in the Western Pacific. Became independent
January 31, 1968.

Capital: Yaren 0S32 166E55

1921 1/15 Adopted S.T. Meridian 172E30
No Daylight Saving Time

NAVARRE See Spain

NEGRI SEMBILAN See Malaya

NEJD See Saudia Arabia

NEPAL
> Constitutional monarchy between China and India
> > Capital: Katmandu 27N43 85E19

> S.T. Meridian 82E30
> > No Daylight Saving Time

NETHERLANDS
> Kingdom in Western Europe
> > Capital: Amsterdam 52N23 4E53

Gregorian Calendar adopted by large cities:
1582	12/15	Holland, Zeeland, Brabant, Vlaandern
1700	6/30	Gelderland
1700	11/30	Utrecht, Overijisol
1700	12/31	Friesland, Groningen
		(no dates for Drente and Limburg Provinces)
1701	1/12	Gregorian Calendar had been adopted nationwide.

To 1846		Local Mean Time
1846		Some large cities introduced Amsterdam time 4E53
1892 5/1		Adopted S.T. Meridian 4E53 except: railroads and some harbors used Greenwich Time 0E00; and some rural regions remained on Local Mean Time.*
1909 5/1		Most of the country on S.T. Meridian 4E53.*

*NOTE: From 1892, 4/1 to 1937 7/1 every city and community used its own time. Therefore for these dates check with local authorities.

1937 7/1	0 hr	Adopted 20 minutes east of Greenwich.
1940 5/16	2 am	Adopted S.T. Meridian 15E00

DAYLIGHT SAVING TIME OBSERVED

1916 5/1 2 am - 10/1 3 am	1928 5/15 2 am - 10/7 3 am
1917 4/16 2 am - 9/17 3 am	1929 5/15 2 am - 10/6 3 am
1918 4/1 2 am - 9/30 3 am	1930 5/15 2 am - 10/5 3 am
1919 4/7 2 am - 9/29 3 am	1931 5/15 2 am - 10/4 3 am
1920 4/5 2 am - 9/27 3 am	1932 5/22 2 am - 10/2 3 am
1921 4/4 2 am - 9/26 3 am	1933 5/15 2 am - 10/8 3 am
1922 3/26 2 am - 10/8 3 am	1934 5/15 2 am - 10/7 3 am
1923 6/1 2 am - 10/7 3 am	1935 5/15 2 am - 10/6 3 am
1924 3/30 2 am - 10/5 3 am	1936 5/15 2 am - 10/4 3 am
1925 6/5 2 am - 10/4 3 am	1937 5/22 2 am - 10/3 3 am
1926 5/15 2 am - 10/3 3 am	1938 5/15 2 am - 10/2 3 am
1927 5/15 2 am - 10/2 3 am	1939 5/15 2 am - 10/8 3 am

Netherlands (*continued*)

1940 5/19 2 am through	hoven 9/20 at 2 pm; Heerlen 9/21 at 3 am;
1942 11/2 3 pm	Sittard Weert 9/22 at 3 am; Helmond 9/26
1943 3/29 2 pm 10/4 3 am	at 8 am; Zalt-Bommel 1945, 5/6 at 8 am.
1944 4/3 2 pm - 10/2 3 am	
1945 4/2 2 pm - 9/16 3 am	

The Allies abolished DST earlier in the south of the country: Maastricht 9/9 at 3 am; Sas van Gent 9/19 at 9 am; Eind-

(Begins 2 AM ends 3 AM)

1977	4/3 - 9/25	1983	3/27 - 9/25
1978	4/2 - 9/30	1984	3/25 - 9/30
1979	4/1 - 9/29	1985	3/31 - 9/29
1980	4/6 - 9/27	1986	3/30 - 9/28
1981	3/29 - 9/27	1987	3/29 - 9/27
1982	3/28 - 9/26	1988	3/27 - 9/25
		1989	3/26 - 9/24
		1990	3/25 - 9/30

NETHERLANDS ANTILLES See Aruba, Bonaire, Curacao, Saba, Saint Eustatius, Sint Marten

NETHERLANDS EAST INDIES

Former Dutch possession (Batavia) located in Southeast Asia.. See **Indonesia**

Capital: Djarkata (Djokjakarta)   6S09 106E49

To 1932   Local Mean Time
1932 11/1 Divided into six time zones as follows:

Netherlands Indies Zone No. 1   S.T. Meridian   135E00
___

MOLUCCAS — Hollandia, Jappen Group, Larat, Manokwari, Schouten Island, Serang, South Diguel, South New Guinea (Papua)

Netherlands Indies Zone No. 2   S.T. Meridian   127E30
___

MOLUCCAS — Ceram and the small islands between New Guinea and Celebes

Netherlands Indies Zone No. 3   S.T. Meridian   120E00
___

CELEBES — Dependencies and Manado Residency

Netherlands Indies Zone No. 4   S.T. Meridian   112E30
___

BORNEO — South and East Division, West Division
    Pontianak, Kalimantan (West Division) 0S02 109E20
       To 1940 Local Mean Time of 109E15
          1940 Changed Meridian to 112E30

JAVA — Bali, Lombok and Madura
    1908 5/1   Local Mean Time of Batavia 110E16
    1924 1/1   S.T. Meridian 110E00
    1932 11/1 S.T. Meridian 112E30

Netherlands Indies Zone No. 5   S.T. Meridian   105E00
___

SOUTH SUMATRA — Benkulen Residency, Bangka and Dependencies, Billiton Asst. Residency, Djambi Residency, Lampongs District Residency, Palenbang Residency, Riouw Residency and Dependencies

Netherlands Indies Zone No. 6   S.T. Meridian   97E30
___

Netherlands East Indies (*continued*)

    NORTH SUMATRA — Governate Acheen and Dependencies, Governate East Coast Sumatra, Residency West Coast Sumatra, Residency Tapanoeli

To 1932	Both North and South Sumatra used Local Mean Time of Padang 100E22
1932 11/1	S.T. Meridian 97E30 assigned to North Sumatra and S.T. Meridian 105E00 assigned to South Sumatra. However, neither was in general use until 1939.
1942 4/1 - 1945 11/17	Entire Netherlands East Indies using S.T. Meridian 135E00 during Japanese occupation
1945 11/17 - 1948 5/1	Gradual return to old time zones
1948 5/1 - 1950 5/1	Territory divided into three time zones:

        (1)   *S.T. Meridian 105E00*
             Bangka, Linga–Archipelago, Riouw–Archipelago, Sumatra and West Coast Islands

        (2)   *S.T. Meridian 120E00*
             Java, Billiton, Celebes, Madura, the islands of Sangihe and Talaud and Soemba

        (3)   *S.T. Meridian 135E00*
             (a)   The Soemba Island Timor and its Northern Islands *until 1949 2/1*
             (b)   Molukken and New Guinea

1950 5/1   Indonesia divided into the following six time zones:

        (1)   *S.T. Meridian 135E00*
             Serang and the Aru-Islands, Hollandia, Irian (former South and West New Guinea), Larat, Manokwari, Saumlaki, Schouten Islands, Tanah Mirah (Upper Diguel), Tanimbar

        (2)   *S.T. Meridian 127E30*
             Molukken (except Larat and Saumlaki, the islands of Aru and Kei), Ceram

        (3)   *S.T. Meridian 120E00*
             Celebes, Flores, Sangihe, Soemba, Soembawa, Talaud, Timor and surrounding islands

        (4)   *S.T. Meridian 112E30*
             Bali, Borneo, Lombok, and Madura. Java, Local Mean Time of Batavia — 106E45

        (5)   *S.T. Meridian 105E00*
             Bangka, Benkoelen, Billiton, Djambi, Enggano, Lampongs, Palembang, and Riouw

Netherlands East Indies (*continued*)

(6)   *S.T. Meridian 97E30*
Sumatra and islands west of it (except Benkoelen, Djambi,
Enggano, Lampongs, Palembang and Riouw)

NETHERLANDS GUIANA   See Surinam

NETHERLANDS NEW GUINEA
Netherlands colony in East Indies
Capital: Manokwari 0S52 134E05

S.T. Meridian 135E00

No Daylight Saving Time

NETHERLANDS TIMOR   See Netherlands East Indies

NETHERLANDS WEST INDIES   See Netherlands Antilles

NEVIS ISLAND
British associate state in the West Indies
Capital: Charlestown 17N08 62W37

To 1912   Local Mean Time
1912 3/2   S.T. Meridian 60W00
No Daylight Saving Time

NEW BRITAIN   See New Guinea

NEW CALEDONIA AND DEPENDENCIES
French colony in South Pacific
Capital: Noumea 22S16 166E28

To 1912   Local Mean Time of Noumea 166E28
1912 1/13 Adopted S.T. Meridian 165E00
DAYLIGHT SAVING TIME OBSERVED
1977 12/4 - 1978 2/27   1978 12/3 - 1979 2/27
1981 - 85 No DST
NEW GEORGIA   See British Solomon Islands   1986 - 90 No DST

NEW GUINEA
Mandated territory under Commonwealth of Australia. Formerly German colonies
Capital: Rabaul 4S12 152E12

Northeastern New Guinea
Capital: Nugima, New Hanover 2S27 150E40

1912   10/1 Adopted S.T. Meridian 150E00
No Daylight Saving Time

New Guinea (*continued*)

    Bismarck Archipelago (former Australian mandate)
New Britain   Capital: Rabaul 4S12 152E12
New Ireland   Capital: Kawieng 2S34 150E49
Admiralty Islands   Capital: Lorungau 2S01 147E17

1912   10/1 Adopted S.T. Meridian 150E00
                        No Daylight Saving Time

    Solomon Islands   Capital: Kieta 6S11 155E40

1912   10/1 Adopted S.T. Meridian 165E00.
                        No Daylight Saving Time

NEW HANOVER See New Guinea

NEW HEBRIDES
    British/French condominium in South Pacific
          Capital: Port Villa 17S44 168E18

    1912 1/13 Adopted S.T. Meridian 165E00
                     No Daylight Saving Time

NEW IRELAND See New Guinea

NEW NANTUCKET ISLAND See Gilbert Islands

NEW SOUTH WALES See Australia

NEW YORK ISLAND See Gilbert Islands

NEW ZEALAND
    British dominion in South Pacific
            Capital: Wellington 41S18 174E47

1752 9/14 Adopted Gregorian calendar

1868 1/1   Adopted S.T. Meridian 172E30
1946 1/1   Adopted S.T. Meridian 180E00

DAYLIGHT SAVING TIME OBSERVED
(changes at 2 am)

Add 1 hr	*Add ½ hr*
1927 11/6 - 1928 3/4	1930 10/12 - 1931 3/15
	1931 10/11 - 1932 3/20
Add ½ hr	1932 10/9 - 1933 3/19
1928 10/14 - 1929 3/17	1933 10/8 - 1934 4/29
1929 10/13 - 1930 3/16	1934 9/30 - 1935 4/28

New Zealand (*continued*)

Add ½ hr	Add 1 hr	
1935 9/29 - 1936 4/26	1974 10/27 - 1975 3/2	1981 10/25 - 1982 3/6
1936 9/27 - 1937 4/25	1975 10/26 - 1976 3/7	1982 10/31 - 1983 3/5
1937 9/26 - 1938 4/24	1976 10/31 - 1977 3/6	1983 10/30 - 1984 3/3
1938 9/25 - 1939 4/30	1977 10/30 - 1978 3/5	1984 10/28 - 1985 3/2
1939 9/24 - 1940 4/28	1978 10/29 - 1979 3/4	1985 10/27 - 1986 3/1
1940 9/29 - 1946 1/1 (year round)	1979 10/28 - 1980 3/2	1986 10/26 - 1987 3/7
1947 - 1973 Not observed	1980 10/26 - 1981 3/1	1987 10/25 - 1988 3/5
		1988 10/30 - 1989 3/4
		1989 10/29 - 1990 3/3
		1990 10/28 - 1991 3/2

NICARAGUA

Republic in Central America

Capital: Managua 12N08 86W18

To 1934	Local Mean Time of Managua 86W18
1934 6/23	Adopted S.T. Meridian 90W00

DAYLIGHT SAVING TIME OBSERVED

1979 3/18 - 6/25   1980 3/16 - 6/23

NICOBAR ISLANDS

With Andaman Islands, form a province of India, located in the Indian Ocean

Capital: Nankauri 8N02 93E32

1920s Adopted S.T. Meridian 97E30 (date unconfirmed)

No Daylight Saving Time

NIGER

Formerly two provinces (Eastern and Western Niger) of French West Africa. Western Niger became independent August 3, 1960. Eastern Niger became independent October 1, 1960.

Capital: Niamey 13N31 2E07

1912 1/1	Western Niger adopted S.T. Meridian 0E00
1934 2/26	Eastern Niger adopted S.T. Meridian 15E00

No Daylight Saving Time

NIGERIA

Federation in West Africa. Former British colony and protectorate. Became independent October 1, 1960

Capital: Lagos 6N27 3E23

1919 9/1 Adopted S.T. Meridian 15E00

No Daylight Saving Time

NINGSIA-HUI See China

NINTAO ISLAND See Tuvalu

NIPPON See Japan

NIUE ISLAND See Savage Island

NON-FEDERATED MALAY STATES See Malaya

NORFOLK ISLAND
Australian territory in South Pacific
Capital: Kingston 29S04 167E58

S.T. Meridian 168E00

No Daylight Saving Time

NORTH BORNEO See British North Borneo

NORTH EAST NEW GUINEA See New Guinea

NORTHERN IRELAND See Great Britain

NORTHERN RHODESIA See Rhodesia

NORTHERN SHAN TERRITORIES See Burma

NORTHERN TERRITORY See Australia

NORTH SUMATRA See Netherlands East Indies

NORWAY
Kingdom in Northern Europe
Capital: Oslo 59N55 10E44

To 1834   Sun Time
1834   Local Mean Time
1895 1/1 Adopted S.T. Meridian 15E00

DAYLIGHT SAVING TIME OBSERVED
(Begins 2 am; ends 3 am)

1916 5/22 - 9/30	1959 3/15 - 9/20	1981 3/29 - 9/26
1917 - 1939 Not observed	1960 3/20 - 9/18	1982 3/28 - 9/25
1940 8/11 - 1942 11/2	1961 3/19 - 9/17	1983 3/25 - 9/29
1943 3/29 - 10/4	1962 3/18 - 9/16	1984 3/31 - 9/28
1944 4/3 - 9/17	1963 3/17 - 9/15	1985 3/31 - 9/27
1945 4/2 - 10/1	1964 3/15 - 9/20	1986 3/30 - 9/28
1946 - 1958 Not observed	1965 4/25 - 9/19	1987 3/29 - 9/27
	1980 4/6 - 9/28	1988 3/27 - 9/25
		1989 3/26 - 9/24
		1990 3/25 - 9/30

NOSSI-BE See Madagascar

NOUVELLE GALLES DU SUD See New South Wales

NOUVELLE HEBRIDES See New Hebrides

NOUVELLE ZELANDE   See New Zealand

NOUVELLE ZEMBLE   See Soviet Union

NOVAYA ZEMLYA   See Soviet Union

NUBIA   See Anglo-Egyptian Sudan and Egypt

NUI ISLAND   See Tuvalu

NUKULAELAE ISLAND   See Tuvalu

NYASALAND
> Former British protectorate in East Africa
> > Capital: Zomba 15S23 35E18
>
> S.T. Meridian 30E00
> > > No Daylight Saving Time
>
> See also Malawi

OCEANIA
> French possession in South Pacific
>
> 1912 10/1 Adopted S.T. Meridian 150W00

OCEAN ISLAND   See Gilbert Islands

OKINAWA ISLAND   See Japan

OMAN, SULTANATE
> Independent monarchy on the Arabian Peninsula. Formerly called Muscat and Oman.
> > Capital: Muscat 23N37 58E37
>
> S.T. Meridian 60E00, but commonly watches are set to midnight at sunset
> > No Daylight Saving Time

ORANGE FREE STATE   See Union of South Africa

ORKNEY ISLANDS   See Great Britain

OSTPREUSSEN   See Germany

OUBANGI–CHARI   See French Equatorial Africa

OUTER MONGOLIA   See Mongolian People's Republic

PAHANG   See Malaya

PAKISTAN
> Formerly part of India. Became a sovereign nation August 15, 1947 and declared itself a
> republic on March 23, 1956.
> > Capital: Islamabad 33N43 75E17

Pakistan (*continued*)
See India for time information prior to 1947.
1947 to 1951 Observed S.T. Meridian 97E30 for civil purposes and 82E30 for railways, postal works, etc.
1951 9/30 Two time zones established:
East Pakistan adopted S.T. Meridian 90E00
Dacca 23N43 90E25
West Pakistan adopted S.T. Meridian 75E00
Karachi 24N52 67E02
No Daylight Saving Time

PALAU See South Seas Mandated Territories

PALESTINE
Former British mandated territory. Now Israel. Became independent May 14, 1948.
Capital: Jerusalem 31N47 35E10
Diplomatic Capital: Tel Aviv 32N04 34E46
To 1918 Local Mean Time of Jerusalem 35E10
1918 S.T. Meridian 30E00

DAYLIGHT SAVING TIME OBSERVED
(Changes at 0 hr)

1940 6/1 - 1942 11/1	1945 4/16 - 11/1 2 am
1943 4/1 2 am - 11/1	1946 4/16 2 am - 11/1
1944 4/1 11/1	1947 Not observed

For later dates, see Israel

PANAMA
Republic between Central and South America
Capital: Panama City 8N57 79W32

To 1908 Local Mean Time of Colon 79W54
1908 4/22 0 hr Adopted S.T. Meridian 75W00
(Natives continued Local Mean Time until 1910)

PAPUA
Former Australian territory in East Indies. Became independent September 17, 1975.
Capital: Port Moresby 9S27 147E08

To 1895 Local Mean Time of Port Moresby 147E08
1895 S.T. Meridian 150E00
No Daylight Saving Time

PARAGUAY
Republic in South America
Capital: Asuncion 25S16 57W41

To 1931 Local Mean Time of Asuncion 57W41
1931 10/10 Adopted S.T. Meridian 60W00

1981 10/1 - 1982 3/31	1986 10/1 - 1987 3/31
1982 10/1 - 1983 3/31	1987 10/1 - 1988 3/31
1983 10/1 - 1984 3/31	1988 10/1 - 1989 3/31
1984 10/1 - 1985 3/31	1989 10/1 - 1990 3/31
1985 10/1 - 1986 3/31	1990 10/1 - 1991 3/31

DAYLIGHT SAVING TIME OBSERVED
1977 10/1 - 1978 2/28   1978 10/1 - 1979 2/28   1979 10/1 - 1980 4/1

PATAGONIA See Argentina

PAYS–BAS See Netherlands

PELELIU ISLAND See South Sea Mandated Territories

PEMBA ISLAND
In the Indian Ocean east of Tanzania

S.T. Meridian 36E00

No Daylight Saving Time

PENANG See Malaya

PEOPLE'S REPUBLIC OF CHINA See China

PEOPLE'S REPUBLIC OF CONGO See Congo (Brazzaville)

PERAK See Malaysia

PERIM ISLAND See Yemen, People's Democratic Republic of

PERLIS See Malaya

PERSIA See Iran

PERU
Republic in South America

Capital: Lima 12S03 77W03

To 1908	Local Mean Time of Callao 77W09
1908 7/28	Adopted S.T. Meridian 75W00

DAYLIGHT SAVING TIME OBSERVED
(changes at 0 hr)

1938 1/1 - 1938 4/1	1981 - 85 No DST
1938 9/25 - 1939 3/26	1986 - 90 No DST
1939 9/24 - 1940 3/24	

PESCADORES ISLANDS See Japan

PETIT MARTINIQUE ISLAND See Grenada

PHILIPPINES
Former U.S. territory in Western Pacific Ocean. Became independent republic July 4, 1946.

Former Capital: Manila 14N35 120E59
Present Capital: Quezon City 14N00 122E11

Philippines (continued)

	Islands run from 112E30 to 127E30
To 1899	Local Mean Time
1899 5/11	Adopted S.T. Meridian 120E00 (not all civilians used it immediately)

DAYLIGHT SAVING TIME OBSERVED
(changes at 0 hr)
1936 11/1 - 1937 2/1
1954 4/12 - 1954 7/1

During the Japanese regime underground forces used Daylight Saving Time
for communications only. Civilians did not observe it.

PHOEBE ISLAND See Gilbert Islands

PHOENIX GROUP See Gilbert Islands

PITCAIRN ISLAND
British colony in South Pacific
Capital: Adamstown 25S00 130W05
S.T. Meridian 150W00

PODKARPATSKA See Czechoslovakia

POLAND
Former republic in Europe. Now a communist state.
Capital: Warszawa (Warsaw) 52N14 21E10

Gregorian Calendar adopted:
1582 10/21	(OS) followed by 11/1 (NS)
1918 3/18	(OS) followed by 4/1 (NS) by Russian Poland, or according to another source 2/14 (OS) followed by 3/1 (NS). (Difference may be due to Civil War and two governments.)
1923 May	Adopted by members of the Orthodox Churches.

Note: The date of birth of Poles born in the Russian part of Poland was usually given in two styles. If only one date is known, then the religious denomination should be considered; Catholics and Protestants used New Style, and Orthodoxists, Old Style. If the religion of the person is not known, then it may be safe to presume it to be Roman Catholic.

1981 10/1	Former Austrian Poland adopted S.T. Meridian 15E00
1893 4/1	Former German Poland adopted S.T. Meridian 15E00
1893 4/1	Former Russian Poland adopted two systems:
	(1) S.T. Meridian 21E00 in territories formerly inown as Congress Poland
	(2) S.T. Meridian 30E18 in the remaining parts of former Rissian Poland
1916 5/1	S.T. Meridian 15E00 adopted in the area of German occupation in the Russian part of Poland

DAYLIGHT SAVING TIME OBSERVED

Germany and occupied area
1916 4/30   11 pm - 10/1 1 am
1917 4/16   2 am - 9/17 3 am
1918 4/15   2 am - 9/16 3 am

Austria and occupied area
1916, 1917, 1918, as above
1919 4/28   2 am - 9/29 3 am

Russia and occupied area
(Again there are two versions which might be due to the Civil War, but the first list is more convincing. All dates in New Style.)

1st list (changes 11 pm, 0 hr)
1917 5/13 - 9/13
1918 6/29 - 8/31
1919 Not observed

2nd List (changes at 24 hr)
1917 4/14 - 1918 12/31:
  Double time from 1918 5/31
  to 12/31

The Polish Republic
1918 4/15   2 am - 9/16 3 am
1919 4/15   2 am - 1922 5/31 24h
1922 - 1939 Not observed

WORLD WAR II:
(Dates marking the start of the movement of the fronts: The Soviet established S.T. Meridian 30E00 1939, 9/17; and the Germans re-established S.T. Meridian 15E00 1941, 6/22. Actual dates for any given place should be checked in World War II reference books.)

The Third Reich and annexed area:
*1940 4/1   2 am - 1942 11/1 3 am
 1943 3/29   2 am - 10/4 3 am
*1944 4/3   2 am - 10/7 0 hr

   *General Government differed: Starting time in 1940 was June 23. And in 1944 starting time (as Reich) was November 31 0 hour.

The Polish People's Republic
1945 4/29 0 hr - 11/1 1 am
1946 4/14 0 hr - 10/7 3 am
1947 5/4 2 am - 10/5 3 am
1948 4/17 2 am - 10/3 3 am
1949 4/10 2 am - 10/2 3 am
1950 to 1956 Not observed
   For following, changes: start 1 am, stop 2 am
1957 6/2 - 9/29
1958 3/30 - 10/4
1959 5/31 - 10/4
1960 4/3 - 10/3

Poland (*continued*)

1961 5/28 - 10/1	1981 3/29 - 9/26
1962 5/27 - 9/30	1982 3/28 - 9/25
1963 5/26 - 9/29	1983 3/27 - 9/24
1964 5/31 - 9/27	1984 3/25 - 9/29
1965 to 1976 Not observed	1985 3/31 - 9/28
1977 4/3 - 9/25	1986 3/30 - 9/28
1978 4/2 - 10/1	1987 3/29 - 9/27
1979 4/1 - 9/29	1988 3/27 - 9/25
1980 3/30 - 9/28	1989 3/26 - 9/24
	1990 3/25 - 9/30

POLYNESIA See Society Islands, Marquesas Islands, Tuamotu Archipelago, Gambier Islands and Austral Islands

PONDICHERRY See French Establishments in India

PONDOLAND See Union of South Africa

PONTIANAK, BORNEO See Netherlands East Indies

PORTUGAL

Republic located in Western Europe
Capital: Lisbon 38N43 9W10

1582 10/15 (NS) Adopted Gregorian calendar
1911   Local Mean Time of Lisbon 9W10
1912 1/1   Adopted S.T. Meridian 0W00

DAYLIGHT SAVING TIME OBSERVED

1916 6/17 11 pm - 11/1 1 am	1937 4/3 11 pm - 10/3 0 hr
1917 3/1 11 pm - 10/15 0 hr	1938 3/26 11 pm - 10/2 0 hr
1918 3/1 11 pm - 10/15 0 hr	1939 4/15 11 pm - 11/19 0 hr
1919 3/1 11 pm - 10/15 0 hr	1940 2/24 11 pm - 10/8 0 hr
1920 3/1 11 pm - 10/15 0 hr	1941 4/5 11 pm - 10/6 0 hr
1921 3/1 11 pm - 10/15 0 hr	* 1942 3/14 11 pm - 10/25 0 hour
1922 - 1923 Not observed	* 1943 3/13 11 pm - - 10/31 0 hour
1924 4/16 11 pm - 10/5 0 hr	* 1944 3/11 11 pm - 10/29 0 hour
1925 Not observed	* 1945 3/10 11 pm - 10/28 0 hour
1926 4/17 11 pm - 10/3 0 hr	1946 4/6 11 pm - 10/6 0 hour
1927 4/9 11 pm - 10/2 0 hr	1947 4/6 - 10/5
1928 4/14 11 pm - 10/7 0 hr	1948 4/4 - 10/3
1929 4/20 11 pm - 10/6 0 hr	1949 4/3 - 10/2
1930 Not observed	1950 4/1 - 10/1
1931 4/18 11 pm - 10/4 0 hr	1951 4/2 - 10/7
1932 4/2 11 pm - 10/2 0 hr	1952 4/6 - 10/5
1933 Not observed	1953 4/5 - 10/4
1934 4/7 11 pm - 10/7 0 hr	1954 4/4 - 10/3
1935 3/30 11 pm - 10/6 0 hr	1955 4/3 - 10/2
1936 4/18 11 pm - 10/4 0 hr	1956 4/1 - 10/7
	1957 4/7 - 10/6

1947 - 1966
changes at 2 am

Portugal (continued)

1958 4/6 - 10/5	1963 4/7 - 10/6	(Changes at 0 hour and 2 am)
1959 4/5 - 10/4	1964 4/5 - 10/4	1976 1/1 - 9/26
1960 4/3 - 10/2	1965 4/4 - 10/3	1977 3/27 - 6/25
1961 4/2 - 10/1	1966 3/3 - 12/31	1978 4/1 - 10/1
1962 4/1 - 10/7	1967 through 1975, DST observed year round.	

1979 3/31 - 9/30
1980 4/6 - 9/28
(Begins at 0 hour, ends 1 AM)
1981 3/28 - 9/26
1982 3/27 - 9/25
1983 3/26 - 9/24
1984 3/24 - 9/29
1985 3/23 - 9/28
(Begins 1 AM, ends 2 AM)
1986 3/30 - 7/28
1987 3/29 - 9/27
1988 3/27 - 9/25
1989 3/26 - 9/24
1990 3/25 - 9/30

* DOUBLE SUMMER TIME - changes at 11 pm and 0 hour

1942 4/25 - 8/16	1944 4/22 - 8/27
1943 4/17 - 8/29	1945 4/21 - 8/26

PORTUGUESE EAST AFRICA
Portuguese colony in East Africa
Capital: Lourenco–Marques 25S58 32E35

To	1903		Local Mean Time of Mozambique 40E40
	1903	3/1	S.T. Meridian 30E00

No Daylight Saving Time

See also **Mozambique**

PORTUGUESE GUINEA
Portuguese overseas province in West Africa
Capital: Bisseau 11N51 15W32

To 1911	Local Mean Time of Bolama 15W32
1911 5/26	Adopted S.T. Meridian 15W00

No Daylight Saving Time

See also **Guinea–Bisseau**

PORTUGUESE INDIA
Portuguese colony in Indian sub-continent, including Daman, Diu, and Goa, which were taken by India on December 18, 1961.
Capital: Nova Goa 15N25 74E05

1911 7/18 Adopted S.T. Meridian 82E30, except Macao
1912 1/1 Macao (Macau) 22N11 113E34 adopted S.T. Meridian 120E00

DAYLIGHT SAVING TIME OBSERVED
Before 1961 information unconfirmed

1961 3/19 - 11/5	1968 4/21 - 10/20	1975 4/20 - 10/19
1962 3/18 - 11/4	1969 4/20 - 10/19	1976 4/18 - 10/17
1963 3/17 - 11/3	1970 4/19 - 10/18	1977 4/17 - 10/16
1964 3/22 - 11/1	1971 4/18 - 10/17	1978 4/16 - 10/15
1965 3/21 - 10/31	1972 4/16 - 10/15	1979 4/15 - 10/21
1966 4/17 - 10/16	1973 4/15 - 10/21	1980 4/20 - 10/19
1967 4/16 - 10/22	1974 4/21 - 10/20	

PORTUGUESE TIMOR
Former Portuguese colony in East Indies. Annexed by Indonesia May 3, 1976
Capital: Dili 8S34 125E35

To 1912   Local Mean Time
1912 1/1   Adopted S.T. Meridian 120E00

PORTUGUESE WEST AFRICA
Former Portuguese colony in Africa. Area now composed of independent countries
Capital of Angola: Luanda 8S49 13E14

1912 1/1   Adopted S.T. Meridian 15E00, except the following, where 0E00 was adopted:
Principe Island, San Antonio 1N39 7E25
Sao Thome Island, Sao Thome 0N20 6E43
No Daylight Saving Time

See also **Sao Tome and Principe**

PRINCE'S ISLAND See **Portuguese West Africa**

PRINCIPE ISLAND See **Sao Tome and Principe**

PROVINCE WELLESLEY See **Malaya**

PRUSSIA See **Germany**

QATAR
A peninsula off the Arabian coast, extending into the Persian (Arabian) Gulf. Former British protected state. Became independent September 1, 1971.
Capital: Doha 25N17 51E32
See also **Saudi Arabia**

QUEENSLAND See **Australia**

RAOUL ISLAND See **Kermadec Islands**

RAPA ISLAND See **French Polynesia**

RARATONGA ISLAND See **Cook Islands**

REDONDA ISLAND See **Antiqua**

REPUBLIC OF CAMEROON See **Cameroon**

REPUBLIC OF CHINA See **Taiwan**

REPUBLIC OF MALDIVES See **Maldive Islands**

REPUBLIC OF SOUTH AFRICA See **South Africa**

REPUBLIC OF TOGO   See Togo

REPUBLIQUE DOMINICAINE   See Dominican Republic

REPUBLIQUE FEDERATIVE POPULAIRE DE BULGARIE   See Bulgaria

REPUBLIQUE FEDERATIVE POPULAIRE DE'L ALBANIE   See Albania

REPUBLIQUE ORIENTALE DE L'URUGUAY   See Uruguay

REUNION ISLAND
   French colony in Indian Ocean
                Capital: Saint-Denis   20S52   55E33

   To 1911   Local Mean Time of Saint-Denis   55E33
      1911 6/1   Adopted S.T. Meridian   60E00
                No Daylight Saving Time

RHODESIA
   Located in South Africa

      Northern Rhodesia,   British protectorate — Capital: Livingstone   17S51   25E52
      Southern Rhodesia,   British colony — Capital: Salisbury   17S50   31E03

   To 1903   Local Mean Time
      1903 3/1   Adopted S.T. Meridian   30E00
                No Daylight Saving Time

See also **Zambia**

RIO DE ORO
   Former Spanish province on the northwest coast of Africa, was relinquished to Morocco and Mauritania in February 1976.
                Capital: Villa Cisneros   23N40   15W55

   1934 2/26   S.T. Meridian   15W00
   1960 11/28 S.T. Meridian   0W00
                No Daylight Saving Time

RIO MUNI   See **Equatorial Guinea**

RIOUW–ARCHIPELAGO   See **Netherlands East Indies**

RODRIGUES ISLAND
   Dependency of Mauritius in Indian Ocean
                Capital: Port Mathuria   19S40   63E26

   To 1907   Local Mean Time of Port Mathuria   63E26
      1907 1/1 S.T. Meridian   60E00
                No Daylight Saving Time

ROMANIA

Former kingdom, now a communist state, located in Eastern Europe
Capital: Bucharest 44N26 26E06

1986	3/30 - 9/28
1987	3/29 - 9/27
1988	3/27 - 9/25
1989	3/26 - 9/24
1990	3/25 - 9/30

1919	3/18	Adopted Gregorian Calendar (NS), dropping 13 days
1891	10/1	S.T. Meridian of Bucharest 26E06
1931	7/24	Adopted S.T. Meridian 30E00
1941	Mid-year	S.T. Meridian 15E00
1945	April	S.T. Meridian 30E00

DAYLIGHT SAVING TIME OBSERVED
(Begins 0 hr; ends 1 am)

1932 5/22 - 10/2	1936 4/5 - 10/4	1943 3/29 - 10/4
1933 4/2 - 10/1	1937 4/4 - 10/3	1944 4/3 - 10/8
1934 4/8 - 10/7	1938 4/3 - 10/2	1980 4/5 - 9/27
1935 4/7 - 10/6	1939 4/2 - 10/7	1981 4/5 - 9/26
		1982 4/4 - 9/25
		1983 4/1 - 9/29
		1984 3/31 - 9/28
		1985 ?

ROTUNDA (ROTOUMAH) ISLAND See Fiji Islands

ROUMANIE See Romania

ROYAUME HACHEMITE DE TRANSJORDANIE See Jordan

RUHR TERRITORY See Germany

RUMANIA See Romania

RUS–KARPATSKA See Czechoslovakia

RUSSIA See Soviet Union

RUSSIAN POLAND See Poland

RUSSIAN S.F.S.R. See Soviet Union

RUTHENIA See Czechoslovakia

RWANDA

Formerly part of Belgian Congo in Africa. Became independent republic July 1, 1962.
Capital: Kigali 1S57 30E00

1935	6/1	Adopted S.T. Meridian 30E00

No Daylight Saving Time

RYUKYU ISLANDS See Japan

SAAR BASIN See Germany

SABA
Island in the Netherlands Antilles located at   17N38   63W10

1912 2/12   Local Mean Time of 63W16
1965 1/1   S.T. Meridian 60W00
                              No Daylight Saving Time

SABAH   See Malaysia

SACHSEN   See Germany

SAHARA   See Algeria, French West Africa and **Rio de Oro**

SAINT BARTHELEMY   See Guadeloupe

SAINT CHRISTOPHER
British associate state in the West Indies
                    Capital: Basseterre 17N18   62W43

To 1912   Local Mean Time
   1912 3/2 S.T. Meridian 60W00
                              No Daylight Saving Time

SAINT EUSTATIUS (Eustachius)
Located in the Netherlands Antilles at   17N30   62W59

1912 2/12   Local Mean Time of 63W15
1965 1/1   S.T. Meridian 60W00
                              No Daylight Saving Time

SAINT HELENA AND DEPENDENCIES
With Ascension Island and Tristan de Cunha, a British colony in South Atlantic
                    Capital: Saint Helena 15S57 5W42

Ascension
To 1912   Local Mean Time of 14W25
   1912 1/1 S.T. Meridian 15W00
   1960s   S.T. Meridian 0W00

Saint Helena
To 1912   Local Mean Time of 5W42
   1912 1/1 S.T. Meridian 5W45
   1960s   S.T. Meridian 0W00

Tristan de Cunha
To 1912   Local Mean Time of 12W19
   1912 1/1 S.T. Meridian 15W00
   1960s   S.T. Meridian 0W00

SAINT KITTS   See St. Christopher

SAINT LUCIA ISLAND
British associate state in the West Indies
Capital: Castries 14N01 61W00

To 1912 Local Mean Time of Castries 61W00
1912 S.T. Meridian 60W00
No Daylight Saving Time

SAINT MARIN   See San Marino

SAINT MARTIN   See Guadeloupe

SAINT PIERRE AND MIQUELON
French colony in North Atlantic
Capital: St. Pierre 46N46 56W10

To 1911   Local Mean Time
1911 5/15 S.T. Meridian 60W00
No Daylight Saving Time

SAINT THOMAS   See Sao Tome and Principe

SAINT VINCENT ISLAND
British associate state in the West Indies
Capital: Kingstown 13N09 61W14

To 1912 Local Mean Time of Kingstown 61W14
1912 S.T. Meridian 60W00
No Daylight Saving Time

1981 - 85 No DST
1986 No DST
1987 4/5 - 10/25
1988 4/3 - 10/30
1989 4/2 - 10/29
1990 4/1 - 10/28

SAKHALIN, JAPANESE   See Japan

SAKHALIN, RUSSIAN   See Soviet Union

SALOMON ILES   See British Solomon Islands and New Guinea

SAMOA   See Western Samoa

SANDWICH ISLANDS   See Falkland Islands and Dependencies

SANGIHE   See Netherlands East Indies

SAN MARINO
Republic near Italy   Capital: San Marino 43N56 12E27

S.T. Meridian 15E00
Daylight Saving Time same as Italy

SANTA CRUZ DE TENERIFE   See Canary Islands

SANTA CRUZ, ILE See New Guinea (Solomon Islands)

SAO JOAO BATISTA DE AJUDE See Dahomey

SAO TOME AND PRINCIPE
Former Portuguese African territory. Became independent July 12, 1975
Capital: Sao Tome 0N20 6E43

1912 1/1 S.T. Meridian 0E00
No Daylight Saving Time
See also **Portuguese West Africa**

SARAWAK
Former British protectorate in East Indies. Part of Malaysia since 1963.
Capital: Kuching 1N33 110E21

1926 3/1   Adopted S.T. Meridian 112E30
1933 1/1   S.T. Meridian 120E00

DAYLIGHT SAVING TIME OBSERVED
(20m advance: changes at 0 hr)

1935 through 1942 9/14 - 12/14

SARDEGNE See Italy

SARDINIA See Italy

SAUDI ARABIA
Kingdom on Arabian Peninsula
Royal Capital: Riad (Riyadh) 24N39 46E42
Administrative Capital: Jidda (Jeddah) 21N29 39E11

S.T. Meridian 60E00, but commonly clocks are set to midnight at sunset
No Daylight Saving Time

SAUMLAKI See Netherlands East Indies

SAVAGE ISLAND (NIUE)
New Zealand dependency in the South Pacific
Capital: Alofi 19S02 169W55

S.T. Meridian 170W00

SAVOY See France

SAXONY See Germany

SCHLESIEN See Germany

SCHOUTEN ISLANDS See Netherlands East Indies

SCHWABEN See Germany

SCHWEIZ See Switzerland

SCORESBY SOUND See Greenland

SCOTLAND See Great Britain

SELANGOR See Malaya

SENEGAL
Former province of French West Africa. Became independent republic August 20, 1960.
Capital: Dakar 14N40 17W26

To 1912		Local time by sun dial
1912	1/1 0 hr	S.T. Meridian 15W00
1941	6/1 0 hr	S.T. Meridian 0W00
		No Daylight Saving Time

SERANG See Netherlands East Indies

SERBIA See Yugoslavia

SEYCHELLES
Former British colony, composed of some 86 islands including Mahe and Amirantes in the
Indian Ocean. Became independent June 29, 1976.
Capital: Victoria 4S36 55E28

To 1906	Local Mean Time of Victoria 55E28
1906 6/1	Mahe adopted S.T. Meridian 60E00
1907 1/1	Amirante adopted S.T. Meridian 60E00
	No Daylight Saving Time

SHANSI See China

SHANTUNG See China

SHENSI See China

SHETLAND ISLANDS See Great Britain

SHIKOKU See Japan

SIAM See Thailand

SIBERIA See Soviet Union

SICILY See Italy

SIEBENGUERGEN See **Romania**

SIERRA LEONE
Former British colony and protectorate in West Africa. Became independent April 27, 1961, and a republic April 19, 1971.

Capital: Freetown 8N29 13W12

To 1913   Local Mean Time of Freetown 13W12
1913 6/1   S.T. Meridian 15W00
1961   S.T. Meridian 0W00

DAYLIGHT SAVING TIME OBSERVED
1935 - 1942 40m advance of clocks from June to September

SILESIA See **Germany** or **Poland**

SINGAPORE
Former British Crown colony in South Asia. Formerly part of Malaya. Became independent August 9, 1965.

Capital: Singapore 1N16 103E51

S.T. Meridian 110E00   No Daylight Saving Time
1960s   S.T. Meridian 105E00
1981 12/31 11:30 pm Adopted S.T. Meridian 120E00

SINKIANG–UIGHUR See **China**

SINT MARTEN ISLAND
Netherlands possession in the West Indies

Capital: Philipsburg 17N59 63W10

1912 2/12   Local Mean Time of 63W10
1965 1/1   S.T. Meridian 60W00

No Daylight Saving Time

SLAVONIA See **Yugoslavia**

SLOVAKIA See **Czechoslovakia**

SLOVENIA See **Yugoslavia**

SLOVENSKO See **Czechoslovakia**

SOCIETE, ILES See **French Polynesia**

SOCIETY ISLANDS See **French Polynesia**

SOCOTRA ISLAND See **Yemen, People's Democratic Republic of**

SOEMBA ISLAND See Netherlands East Indies

SOEMBAWA ISLAND See Netherlands East Indies

SOLOMON ISLANDS See New Guinea

SOMALIA
Formerly British and Italian Somaliland (see). Now democratic republic in East Africa.
Became independent July 1, 1960.
Capital: Mogadishu 2N02 45E21

1960 S.T. Meridian 45E00
No Daylight Saving Time

SOMALILAND See British, French or Italian Somaliland

SOMBRERO
British associate state in the West Indies located at 18N35 63W25

To 1911   Local Mean Time
1911 7/1 0:01 am   S.T. Meridian 60W00
No Daylight Saving Time

SOUDAN See French West Africa (French Sudan)

SOUDAN ANGLO-EGYPTIAN See Anglo-Egyptian Sudan

SOUS LE VENT, ILES See Windward Islands

SOUTH AFRICA
Composed of the former British colonies of the Cape of Good Hope, Natal, Orange Free State,
and Transvaal. Became an independent republic May 31, 1961.
Legislative Capital: Cape Town 33S55 18E25
Administrative Capital: Pretoria 25S45 28E11

S.T. Meridian 30E00

See also **Union of South Africa**

SOUTH AUSTRALIA See Australia

SOUTHERN RHODESIA See Rhodesia

SOUTHERN YEMEN See Yemen, People's Democratic Republic of

SOUTH GEORGIA See Falkland Islands and Dependencies

SOUTH SANDWICH ISLANDS See Falkland Islands and Dependencies

SOUTH SEA MANDATED TERRITORIES
Japanese mandated territories (former German possession) in North Pacific. Taken from Japan in World War II.

(1) *Mariana or Iadrone Islands*
> Capital: Tanapag 15N14 145E41

> S.T. Meridian 135E00

(2) *Carolines* (Palau, Peleliu, Truk, Yap)
> Capital: Truk 7N22 151E54

> Divided into 3 zones:
> East of 154E00: S.T. Meridian 165E00
> Between 154E00 and 148E00: S.T. Meridian 150E00
> West of 148E00: S.T. Meridian 135E00

(3) *Marshall Islands* (Bikini, Eniwetok, Kwaylein)
> Capital: Jaluit 5N55 169E38

> S.T. Meridian 165E00
> > No Daylight Saving Time

SOUTHWEST AFRICA See Namibia

SOVIET UNION (U.S.S.R.)
Largest country in the world, stretching across two continents from the North Pacific to the Baltic Sea, has eleven (11) time zones. U.S.S.R. is composed of 15 Soviet Union Republics (S.S.R.) within certain of which are subdivisions called Autonomous Soviet Socialist Republics (A.S.S.R.). Official name: Union of Soviet Socialist Republics, formed at Petrograd (Leningrad), noon, September 15, 1917.
> Capital: Moscow 55N45 37E35

UNION REPUBLICS	Capital	Latitude	Longitude
European			
(1) Armenian S.S.R.	Erivan	40N11	44E30
(2) Azerbaijan S.S.R.	Baku	40N25	49E50
(3) Byelorussian S.S.R.	Minsk	53N50	27E35
(4) Estonian S.S.R.	Tallinn	59N26	24E43
(5) Georgian S.S.R.	Tbilisi	41N45	44E55
(6) Latvian S.S.R.	Riga	56N55	24E07
(7) Lithuanian S.S.R.	Vilna	54N41	25E19
(8) Moldavian S.S.R.	Kishinev	47N00	28E50
(9) Russian S.F.S.R.	Moscow	55N45	37E35
(10) Ukrainian S.S.R.	Kiev	50N27	30E32
Asian			
(11) Kazakh S.S.R.	Alma–Ata	43N12	76E57
(12) Kirghiz S.S.R.	Frunze	42N54	74E36
(13) Tadzhik S.S.R.	Dushanbe	38N34	68E48
(14) Turkmen S.S.R.	Ashkhabad	43N12	76E57
(15) Uzbek S.S.R.	Tashkent	41N20	69E18

Soviet Union (*continued*)
    1918 2/14   Adopted Gregorian Calendar (NS) by dropping 13 days

    19th century dates differ from Gregorian Calendar by 12 days
    20th century dates differ from Gregorian Calendar by 13 days
        Example: When it is September 8 Gregorian (NS), it is August 26 Julian Calendar (OS).

Imperial Russian Time Zones formerly in Use
Riga   56N58   24E05   Local Mean Time in general use
Pulkovo (Leningrad)   59N53   29E54   Local Mean Time, official only
Nicolaeff (Nikolayev)   46N58   32E00   Local Mean Time in general use
Siberia: Irkutsk   52N16   104E20 Local Mean Time in general use
Vladivostok   42N05   131E50 Local Mean Time in general use

1930 6/16   Clocks advanced one hour until:
1931 1/1   Soviet Union rezoned into eleven (11) time zones as follows:

TIME ZONES IN EUROPE

U.S.S.R. Zone No. 1   20E30 to 37E30   S.T. Meridian 45E00

Byelorussian S.S.R.	Kola Peninsula
Central Black Soil Area	Leningrad Area
Crimea	Moldavian S.S.R.
Ivanovo Industrial Area (West)	Moscow Industrial Area
Karelian A.S.S.R.	Ukrainian S.S.R.

U.S.S.R. Zone No. 2   37E30 to 52E30   S.T. Meridian 45E00

Abkhaz A.S.S.R.	Ivanovo Industrial Area (Central)
Adzhar A.S.S.R.	Kalmuck A.S.S.R.
Armenian S.S.R.	Kazak S.S.R. (West)
Azerbaijan S.S.R.	Lower Volga Area
Bashkir S.S.R.	Middle Volga Area
Central Black Soil Area	Nakhichevan A.S.S.R.
Chuvash A.S.S.R.	Nizhni–Novgorod Area
Dagestan A.S.S.R.	N. Caucasian Area
Georgian S.S.R.	Tatar A.S.S.R.
	Ural Area (West)

TIME ZONES IN ASIA

U.S.S.R. Zone No. 3   52E30 to 67E30   S.T. Meridian 60E00

Bashkir A.S.S.R. (East)	Turkmen S.S.R.
Kara Kalpak Area	Ural Area (Central)
Kazakh S.S.R. (Central)	Uzbeck S.S.R.
Tadzhik S.S.R.	

Soviet Union (*continued*)

Time Zones in Asia (*continued*)

U.S.S.R. Zone No. 4	67E30 to 82E30	S.T. Meridian 75E00

Kazakh S.S.R. (East)   Ural Area (East)
Kirghiz S.S.R.   Yamal Peninsula
Siberian Area (West)

U.S.S.R. Zone No. 5	82E30 to 97E30	S.T. Meridian 90E00

Cyrot–Tura Area   Siberian Area (Central)

U.S.S.R. Zone No. 6	97E30 to 112E30	S.T. Meridian 105E00

Buryat-Mongol   Yakutsk A.S.S.R. (West)
Siberian Area (East)

U.S.S.R. Zone No. 7	112E30 to 127E30	S.T. Meridian 120E00

Far Eastern Area (West)   Yakutsk A.S.S.R. (West Central)
Siberian Area (S.E.)

U.S.S.R. Zone No. 8	127E30 to 142E30	S.T. Meridian 135E00

Far Eastern Area (West Central)   Yakutsk A.S.S.R. (Central)

U.S.S.R. Zone No. 9	142E30 to 157E30	S.T. Meridian 150E00

Far Eastern Area (Central)   Yakutsk A.S.S.R. (East Central)

U.S.S.R. Zone No. 10	157E30 to 172E30	S.T. Meridian 165E00

Far Eastern Area (East Central)   Yakutsk A.S.S.R. (East)
Kamchatka

U.S.S.R. Zone No. 11	172E30 to Eastward	S.T. Meridian 180E00

Far Eastern Area

DAYLIGHT SAVING TIME OBSERVED

1917 4/14 - 1918 5/31
Then clocks advanced 1 hour more for rest of 1918
1930 6/16 - 12/31
1941 - 1945 Continuous
Beginning and ending dates not available

1963 All time zones advanced one hour year round

See page 112 for additional time change information.

SPAIN

Kingdom in Western Europe on the Iberian peninsula, including the enclaves of Ceuta and Melilla.

Capital: Madrid 40N25 3W41

1582	10/15	(NS) Adopted Gregorian calendar	
To	1901	Local Mean Time of Madrid 3W41	
1901	1/1	Adopted S.T. Meridian 0W00	
1946	9/30	0 hr Adopted S.T. Meridian 15E00	

DAYLIGHT SAVING TIME OBSERVED

1917 5/5 11 pm - 10/7 0 hr
1918 4/6 11 pm - 10/6 0 hr
1919 4/5 11 pm - 10/5 0 hr
1920 - 1923 Not observed
1924 4/15 11 pm - 10/5 0 hr
1926 4/17 11 pm - 10/3 0 hr
1927 4/9 11 pm - 10/2 0 hr
1928 4/14 11 pm - 10/7 0 hr
1929 4/20 11 pm - 10/6 0 hr

Country split during Spanish Civil War

Zona Republicana

1937 6/16 11 pm - 10/7 0 hr + 1 hour
1938 4/2 11 pm - 4/30 11 pm + 1 hour
4/30 11 pm - 10/3 0 hr + 2 hours
10/2 11 pm - 12/31 24 hr + 1 hour
1939 1/1 0 hr - 4/1 24 hr + 1 hour

Zona De Los Insurrectos (Franco's Side)

1937 5/23 11 pm - 10/3 0 hr + 1 hour
1938 3/26 11 pm - 10/2 0 hr + 1 hour
1939 3/31 11 pm - see below

All of Spain

1939 4/15 11 pm - 1946 9/30 0 hr plus*	1981 3/29 - 9/26
1947 - 1948 Not observed	1982 3/28 - 9/25
1949 4/30 11 pm - 10/3 0 hr	1983 3/25 - 9/29
1950 - 1973 Not observed	1984 3/31 - 9/28
1974 4/13 11 pm - 9/29 0 hr	1985 3/31 - 9/27
1975 - 1976 Not observed	1986 3/30 - 9/28
1977 4/3 11 pm - 9/25 0 hr	1987 3/29 - 9/27
	1988 3/27 - 9/25
1978 4/2 - 9/30	1989 3/26 - 9/24
1979 4/1 - 9/29	1990 3/25 - 9/30
1980 3/30 - 9/28	

*Add 1 more hour for DOUBLE SUMMER TIME
(Begins 11 pm; ends 0 hr)
1942 5/2 - 9/2   1943 4/17 - 10/4   1944 4/15 - 10/11
1945 4/14 - 10/1   1946 4/13 - 9/30

SPANISH GUINEA   See **Equatorial Guinea**

SPANISH MOROCCO
    Former Spanish possession in North Africa, now part of Morocco.
        Capital: Melilla 35N23 3W00

   1901 1/1   Adopted S.T. Meridian 0W00
               The Moors used sun time for years.
   1946 9/30   0 hr Adopted S.T. Meridian 15E00
                     Daylight Saving Time same as **Spain**
                     (See Franco's Side for 1937 - 1939)

SPANISH SAHARA   See **Rio de Oro**

SRI LANKA   See **Ceylon**

ST.   See under **Saint, Sint**

STATE OF VATICAN CITY   See **Vatican City State**

STRAITS SETTLEMENTS   See **Malaya**

SUDAN
    Formerly Anglo–Egyptian Sudan. Became independent January 1, 1956.
        Capital: Khartoum 15N36 32E32

   S.T. Meridian 30E00

DAYLIGHT SAVING TIME OBSERVED
1972 4/30 - 10/15	1975 4/27 - 10/15
1973 4/29 - 10/15	1976 4/25 10/15
1974 4/28 - 10/15	1977 4/24 - 10/15
	1981 - 85 No DST

SUEDE   See **Sweden**

SUISSE   See **Switzerland**

SUMATRA   See **Indonesia**

SUNDAY ISLAND   See **Karmadec Islands**

SUOMI   See **Finland**

SURINAME
    Former Netherlands Guiana on the north coast of South America. Became independent
    November 25, 1976
        Capital: Paramaribo 5N50 55W13

Suriname (*continued*)

To	1911	Local Mean Time
	1911	Local Mean Time of Paramaribo 55W13
	1935	Adopted S.T. Meridian 55W08:35
	1945 10/1	Adopted S.T. Meridian 52W30
	1984 ?	Adopted S.T. Meridian 45W00 No Daylight Saving Time

SWABIA See Germany

SWAZILAND

Former British protectorate in South Africa. Became independent September 6, 1968.
Capital: Mbabane 26S19 31E08

S.T. Meridian 30E00

No Daylight Saving Time

SWEDEN

Kingdom in Northern Europe

Capital: Stockholm 59N20 18E03

1753 3/1	Adopted Gregorian calendar	1916 5/1 - 9/30	(Begins 2 AM, ends 3 AM)	
1879 1/1 0 hr	Adopted S. T. Meridian 15E03 29.8	1917 4/16 - 9/15	1981 3/29 - 9/26	
1900 1/1 1 am	Adopted S.T. Meridian 15E00	1918 4/6 - 9/15	1982 3/28 - 9/25	
		1941 4/8 - 1942 11/1	1983 3/25 - 9/29	
		1943 3/29 - 10/3	1984 3/31 - 9/28	
DAYLIGHT SAVING TIME OBSERVED		1944 4/3 - 10/2		
		1945 5/2 - 11/2	1985 3/31 - 9/27	
1916 5/14 11 p.m. - 10/1 0 hr (Government Only)		1946 3/31 - 10/6	1986 3/30 - 9/28	
1980 4/6 2 am - 9/28 3 am		1947 4/6 -10/5		
		1948 4/4 - 10/4	1987 3/29 - 9/27	
		1949 4/10 - 10/1	1988 3/27 - 9/25	
		1954 5/23 - 10/3		
		1955 5/22 - 10/2	1898 3/26 - 9/24	
		1956 6/3 - 9/30		
		1957 6/2 - 9/29	1990 3/25 - 9/30	
		1991 4/6 - 9/27		

SWITZERLAND

Federal republic in Central Europe

Capital: Bern 46N57 7E28

1584 1/22		Gregorian calendar adopted by Catholic districts including: Lucerne, Schwyz, Solothurn, and Zug.
1701 1/12		Gregorian calendar adopted by Baselstadt, Bern, Genf, Neuchatel, Cargons, Schaffhausen, Thurgau, and Zurich.
1724 1/1		Gregorian calendar adopted by Protestant districts including: Appenzel, Glarus, St. Gallen.
To	1894	Local Mean Time of Bern 7E28
	1894 6/1	Adopted S.T. Meridian 15E00

DAYLIGHT SAVING TIME OBSERVED
(Begins 2 am; ends 0 hr)

1941 5/5 - 10/6   1942 5/4 - 10/5

1981 3/29 - 9/26	Begins 2 AM, ends 3 AM)
1982 3/28 - 9/26	1986 3/30 - 9/28
1983 3/27 - 9/25	1987 3/29 - 9/27
1984 3/25 - 9/30	1988 3/27 - 9/25
1985 3/31 - 9/29	1989 3/26 - 9/24
	1990 3/25 - 9/30

SYRIA

Formerly one of the Levant States located in Western Asia. Became an independent Arab republic January 1, 1944.

Syria (*continued*)

Capital: Damascus 33N30 36E18

1920 Adopted S.T. Meridian 30E00

DAYLIGHT SAVING TIME OBSERVED
(Changes at 2 am)

1920 4/18 - 10/3	1964 4/26 - 11/1	1971 4/25 - 10/1
1921 4/17 - 10/2	1965 4/25 - 9/30	1972 4/30 - 10/1
1922 4/16 - 10/1	1966 4/24 - 9/30	1973 4/29 - 10/1
1923 4/15 - 10/7	1967 4/30 - 10/1	1974 4/28 - 10/1
1924 - 1959 Not observed	1968 4/28 - 10/1	1975 4/27 - 10/1
1962 4/29 - 9/30	1969 4/27 - 10/1	1976 4/25 - 10/1
1963 4/28 - 9/30	1970 4/26 - 10/1	1977 4/24 - 10/1
		1978 5/1 - 8/31

SZECHWAN See China

1981 - 85 No DST
1986 2/16 - 10/19

TADZHIK S.S.R. See Soviet Union

1987 2/22 - 10/18
1988 3/1 - 11/1

1989 3/1 - 11/1

TAHITI See French Polynesia

1990 3/1 - 11/1

TAIWAN REPUBLIC
Official Name: Republic of China. Former Japanese possession returned to China in 1945.
Capital: T'aipei 25N03 121E30

1896 1/1   Adopted S.T. Meridian   120E00

DAYLIGHT SAVING TIME OBSERVED

1945 - 1951 5/1 - 9/30	1960 - 1961 6/1 - 9/30
1952 3/1 - 10/31	1962 - 1973 Not observed
1953 - 1954 4/1 - 10/31	1974 - 1975 4/1 - 9/30
1955 - 1959 4/1 - 9/30	1980 6/30 - 9/30

See also **China**

TALAUD See Netherlands East Indies

TANAH MIRAH See Netherlands East Indies

TANGANYIKA TERRITORY
Former German East Africa and British Mandated Territory in East Africa. Became independent December 9, 1961.
Capital: Dar-es-Salaam 6S50 39E17

By 1931   Using S.T. Meridian 45E00
By 1948   S.T. Meridian 41E15
By 1961   S.T. Meridian 45E00

Tanganyika Territory (*continued*)

No Daylight Saving Time

See also **Tanzania**

TANGIER
Former internationalized seaport in North Africa, controlled by Morocco since 1956.

Capital: Tanger 35N47 5W48

1917 10/26 S.T. Meridian 0W00, but Moors used sun time for years.

DAYLIGHT SAVING TIME OBSERVED
(changes at 11 pm)

1918 5/6 - 10/7	1925 Not observed
1919 - 1923 Not observed	1926 4/17 - 10/2
1924 4/16 - 10/4	1927 4/9 - 10/1
1928 4/14 - 10/6	

TANIMBAR ISLAND See Netherlands East Indies

TANZANIA
Formerly British mandate of Tanganyika and Zanzibar in East Africa. Became a united republic April 26, 1964.

Capital: Dar-es-Salaam 6S50 39E17

S.T. Meridian 41E15

1961 S.T. Meridian 45E00

TASMANIA See Australia

TCHAD See Chad

TCHECOSLOVAQUIE See Czechoslovakia

TENERIFE See Canary Islands

TERNATE See Netherlands East Indies

THAILAND
Kingdom in Southeastern Asia, formerly called Siam

Capital: Bangkok 13N45 100E31

To 1920   Local Mean Time of Bangkok 100E31
    1920   4/1 Adopted S.T. Meridian 105E00
                    No Daylight Saving Time

THULE See Greenland

THURINGIA   See Germany

TIBET   See China

TIBET–CHAMDO   See China

TIMOR   See Netherlands East Indies and Portuguese Timor

TOBAGO   See Trinidad and Tobago

TOGO

Formerly part of French West Africa and Gold Coast. Became independent republic
April 27, 1960.

Capital: Lome   6N08   1E14

1893 Adopted S.T. Meridian   0E00

No Daylight Saving Time

TOKELAU ISLANDS   See Union Islands

TONGA

Native kingdom under British protectorate. Located in South Pacific. Became independent
June 4, 1970

Capital: Nukualofa   21S08   175W12

S.T. Meridian   175W00

1931 Friendly Islands (Iles Amis) using Local Mean Time of   167W40

TONKIN   See French Indo–China

TORRES ISLAND   See New Hebrides

TOSCANA   See Italy

TRANSJORDAN   See Jordan

TRANSKEI

Republic on the east coast of South Africa. Became independent October 26, 1976.
Capital: Umtata   28E47   31S35

1984 9/1   S.T. Meridian 30E00

TRANSVAAL   See Union of South Africa

TRANSYLVANIA   See Romania

TRENGGANU   See Malaya

TRINIDAD AND TOBAGO
Former British colony in Lesser Antilles. Became independent August 31, 1962.
Capital: Port of Spain   10N39   61W31

1912 3/?   Adopted S.T. Meridian   60W00
No Daylight Saving Time

TRINITE See British West Indies and Brazil

TRIPOLIS See Libya

TRIPOLITANA See Libya

TRISTAN DE CUNHA   See St. Helena

TRUCIAL COAST   See Saudi Arabia

TRUK ISLAND   See South Seas Mandated Territories

TSINGHAI See China

TUAMOTU ARCHIPELAGO   See French Polynesia

TUBUAI ISLANDS   (Austral) See French Polynesia

TUNISIA
Formerly regency under French administration in North Africa. Became an independent
republic March 20, 1956.

			1981 - 85 No DST
	Capital: Tunis 36N48 10E10		1986 5/26 - 9/28
			1987 5/29 - 9/27
			1988 5/30 - 9/25
To	1881	Legal time was Moslem Time — sunset to sunrise	1898 5/29 - 9/24
	1881 5/12	Local Mean Time of Paris 2E20	1990 5/28 - 9/30
	1911 3/9	Adopted S.T. Meridian 15E00	

Daylight Saving Time after 1939 may have been the same as France

TURKESTAN   See Soviet Union

TURKEY
Republic located in Europe and Asia
Capital until 1922: Istanbul   41N01   28E58
Capital after 1922: Ankara   39N57   32E50

1908	Europeans adopted Gregorian calendar
1917	Asians adopted Gregorian calendar
1880	Local Mean Time of Santa Sophia Cathedral in Istanbul 28E58
1910 10/1	Adopted S.T. Meridian 30E00, but two kinds of time were used: Turkish time (Local Mean Time of Santa Sophia 28E58) and 30E00 for the Europeans. Both times used by railways. Trains ran on 30E00 and time

Turkey (*continued*)

tables were in Turkish time. Official clocks were set each day to read noon by the sunrise method, but tower clocks, set on 30E00, were adjusted twice a week.

DAYLIGHT SAVING TIME OBSERVED
(In Istanbul only)

1916 5/1 - 10/1	1921 4/3 - 10/3	1981 - 85 No DST
1920 3/28 - 10/25	1922 3/26 - 10/8	1986 3/30 - 9/28
	1940s Observed, no dates	1987 3/29 - 9/27
		1988 3/27 - 9/25
		1989 3/26 - 9/24
		1990 3/25 - 9/30

TURKMEN S.S.R. See Soviet Union

TURKS ISLANDS See Jamaica

TURQUES, ILES See Jamaica

TURQUIE See Turkey

TUSCANY See Italy

TUVALU

Formerly the Ellice Islands. A group of nine islands, including Funafuti, Nanumea, Nukufetau, Nurakita, Nui, Nukulaelae, and Vaitupu islands
Capital: Fongafak, Funafuti 8S31 179E13

S.T. Meridian 180E00

No Daylight Saving Time

UGANDA

Former British protectorate in East Africa. Became independent October 9, 1962, and a republic October 9, 1963.
Former Capital: Entebbe 0N03 32E34
New Capital: Kampala 0N19 32E14

To 1928		Local Mean Time	
	1928 6/31 0 hr	Adopted S.T. Meridian 45E00	
	1930 1/1 0 hr	Adopted S.T. Meridian 37E30	
By 1948		S.T. Meridian 41E15 (adoption date unknown)	

No Daylight Saving Time

UKRAINIAN S.S.R. See Soviet Union

ULSTER See Northern Ireland under Great Britain

UNION DE L'AFRIQUE DU SUD See Union of South Africa

UNION DES REPUBLIQUES SOVIETIQUES SOCIALISTES See Soviet Union

UNION ISLANDS (Tokelau)
    In the Pacific Ocean southwest of Hawaii. Administered by New Zealand.

    1911 S.T. Meridian 172W30

UNION OF SOUTH AFRICA
    Legislative union of self-governing British colonies in South Africa.
          Capital: Pretoria 25S45 28E11

    To 1892 Local Mean Time

Cape Colony Province
    1892 2/8 Adopted S.T. Meridian 22E30
    1903 3/1 Adopted S.T. Meridian 30E00

Cape of Good Hope
    1892 2/8 Adopted S.T. Meridian 22E30
    1903 3/1 Adopted S.T. Meridian 30E00

Natal
    To 1894   Durban Observatory Time 31E03
    1894 9/1 Adopted S.T. Meridian 30E00

Orange Free State
    To 1892   Local Mean Time of Bloemfontein 26E13
    1892 2/8 Adopted S.T. Meridian 22E30
    1903 3/1 Adopted S.T. Meridian 30E00

Transvaal
    1892 2/8 Adopted S.T. Meridian 22E30
    1903 3/1 Adopted S.T. Meridian 30E00

    By 1903 3/1 All of union was observing S.T. Meridian 30E00

DAYLIGHT SAVING TIME OBSERVED
(changes at 2 am)

1942 7/27 - 1943 3/21	Natal
1942 9/20 - 1943 3/21	Transvaal, Orange Free State, Cape Province Southwest Africa
1943 9/19 - 1944 3/19	All of the Union of South Africa, including High Commission Territories, Swaziland, Basutoland and Bechuanaland, except Southwest Africa

UNION OF SOVIET SOCIALIST REPUBLICS See Soviet Union

UNITED ARAB EMIRATES
Former British protected states stretching 400 miles along the Persian (Arabian) Gulf. Became independent December 2, 1971. (See Saudi Arabia)
Capital: Abu Dhabi   24N30   54E28

Time not standardized

UNITED KINGDOM See Great Britain

UNITED REPUBLIC OF TANZANIA See Tanzania

UPPER SENEGAL See Senegal

UPPER VOLTA
Formerly part of French West Africa. Became an independent republic August 5, 1960.
Capital: Ouagadougou   12N22   1W31

1912 1/1   Adopted S.T. Meridian   0W00

URAL AREA See Soviet Union

URUGUAY
Republic in South America
Capital: Montevideo   34S53   56W10

1898 6/28   0 hr Adopted Local Mean Time of Montevideo   56W10
1920 5/1   0 hr Adopted S.T. Meridian   52W30
1942 12/14   0 hr Adopted S.T. Meridian   45W00

DAYLIGHT SAVING TIME OBSERVED
(changes at 0 hr)

NOTE: ½ hour increase only

Montevideo only
1923 10/2 - 1924 4/1   1925 10/1 - 1926 4/1
1924 10/1 - 1925 4/1   1927 - 1932 Not observed

Entire Country
1933 10/29 - 1934 4/1   1937 10/31 - 1938 3/27
1934 10/28 - 1936 4/1   1938 10/30 - 1939 3/26
1935 10/27 - 1936 3/30   1939 10/29 - 1940 3/31
1936 11/1 - 1937 3/28   1940 10/27 - 1941 3/30
1941 8/1 - 1942 1/1

NOTE: 1 hour increase on following

1942 12/14 - 1943 3/14   1944 - 1958 Not observed

Uruguay (*continued*)

1959 5/24 - 1959 11/15	1965 4/4 - 1965 9/26
1960 1/17 - 1960 3/6	1966 - 1971 Not observed
1961 - 1964 Not observed	1972 April to Mid-August (power shortage)
1973 - 1977 Not observed	

URUNDI See Burundi

U.S.S.R. See Soviet Union

UVEA ISLAND See New Caledonia

UZBEK S.S.R. See Soviet Union

VAITUPU ISLAND See Tuvalu

VATICAN CITY, ETAT DU See **Vatican City State**

VANUATU

Located in SW Pacific,
1200 miles NE of Brisbane Australia
Became a republic July 30, 1980
Capital: Villa   17S44   168E18
Standard time meridian: 165E00
No Daylight Savings Time.

VATICAN CITY STATE

Located in the City of Rome, Italy

Vatican Observatory 41N54 12E27

1893 11/1   0 hr Adopted S.T. Meridian 15E00

Daylight Saving Time not confirmed, perhaps the same as Rome, Italy

1981 3/29 - 9/26	(Begins 2 AM, ends 3 AM)
1982 3/28 - 9/25	1986 3/30 - 9/28
1983 3/25 - 9/29	1987 3/29 - 9/27
1984 3/31 - 9/28	1988 3/27 - 9/25
1985 3/31 - 9/27	1989 3/26 - 9/24
	1990 3/25 - 9/30

VENEZUELA

Republic in South America

Capital: Caracas 10N30 66W55

To 1912 Local Mean Time of Caracas 66W55
1912 2/12   S.T. Meridian 67W30
1965 1/1   0:30 am Adopted S.T. Meridian 60W00

No Daylight Saving Time.

Sunset varies only 30 to 45 minutes during the entire year

VICTORIA See Australia

VIETNAM, NORTH

Formerly French Indo–China. Became Democratic Republic of Vietnam June 4, 1954.
Reunited with South Vietnam to become Socialist Republic of Vietnam July 2, 1976.

Capital: Hanoi 21N01 105E50

1912 5/1   S.T. Meridian 120E00
1931 5/1   S.T. Meridian 105E00

No Daylight Saving Time

See also **French Indo China**

VIETNAM, SOUTH
Formerly French Indo-China. Became Republic of Vietnam December 29, 1954.
Reunited with North Vietnam to become Socialistic Republic of Vietnam July 2, 1976.
Capital: Saigon 10N47 106E35

1906 6/9   Local Mean Time of 106E35

No Daylight Saving Time

See also **French Indo China**

VIRGIN ISLANDS
British possession in the Caribbean Sea
Capital: Roadtown, Tortola 18N27 64W37

To 1911   Local Mean Time
1911 7/1   0:01 am S.T. Meridian 60W00
No Daylight Saving Time

VOLCANO ISLANDS See **Japan**

VOLGA AREA See **Soviet Union**

WALES See **Great Britain**

WALLACHIA See **Romania**

WALLIS AND FUTUNA ISLANDS
French protectorate in South Pacific
Capital: Mata-Utu 13S17 176W08

S.T. Meridian 180W00

WALVIS BAY See **Union of South Africa**

WASHINGTON ISLAND See **Gilbert Islands**

WELLESLEY PROVINCE See **Malaya**

WESTERN AUSTRALIA See **Australia**

WESTERN NIGER See **Niger**

WESTERN SAMOA
Formerly British mandate, administered by New Zealand in South Pacific. Became
independent January 1, 1962.
Capital: Apia 13S49 171W46

Western Samoa (*continued*)
To 1911 Local Mean Time of Apia 171W46
1911 S.T. Meridian 172W30
Same Daylight Saving Time as **New Zealand**

WEST GERMANY See Germany, West

WEST INDIES
Greater Antilles: **See Cuba, Dominican Republic, Haiti, Jamaica**
Lesser Antilles: **See Aruba, Bonaire, Curacao, Leeward Islands, Windward Islands**

WEST IRIAN See Netherlands East Indies

WEST MALAYSIA See Malaysia

WEST PAKISTAN See Pakistan

WHITE RUSSIAN S.S.R. See Soviet Union

WINDWARD ISLANDS See Aruba, Barbados, Bonaire, Curacao, Dominica, Grenada, Grenadines, Martinique, St. Lucia, St. Vincent

WRANGEL ISLANDS See Soviet Union

YAEYAMA ISLANDS See Japan

YAMAL PENINSULA See Soviet Union

YANAON See French Establishments in India

YAP See South Sea Mandated Territories

YEMEN, ARAB REPUBLIC OF
Located at the southern tip of the Arabian Peninsula on the Red Sea. Became independent November 30, 1967.
Capital: Sanao 15N23 44E13

Time not standardized

YEMEN, PEOPLE'S DEMOCRATIC REPUBLIC OF
Located on the Arabian Sea and Gulf of Aden. Consists of states, sultanates, and sheikdoms formerly ruled by the British. Also the islands of Kamaran, Perim, and Socotra. Became independent November 30, 1967.
Capitals: Aden 12N47 45E02
Medina as-Shaab 24N30 39E45

Time not standardized

YUGOSLAVIA

Formerly Kingdom of Serbs, Croates, and Slovenes. Now a communist state.

Capital: Belgrade 44N49 20E27

1919	Adopted Gregorian Calendar
1884	S.T. Meridian 15E00 adopted by Serbia and extended to Yugoslavia when new state was formed.
1891 10/1	Serbia legalized S.T. Meridian 15E00

DAYLIGHT SAVING TIME OBSERVED

1941 - 1944 Same as Germany

1981	No DST	1986	3/30 - 9/28
1982	No DST	1987	3/29 - 9/27
1983	3/25 - 9/29	1988	3/27 - 9/25
1984	3/31e - 9/28e	1989	3/26 - 9/24
1985	?	1990	3/25 - 9/30

YUNNAN See China

ZAIRE

Republic in Equatorial Africa. On October 27, 1971, changed its name from Congo to Zaire.

Capital: Kinshasa 48S19 15E00

S.T. Meridian 15E00

No Daylight Saving Time

See also Congo and Congo (Kinshasa)

ZAMBIA

Formerly Northern Rhodesia in Africa. Became independent republic October 24, 1964.

Capital: Lusaka 15S25 28E18

1903 3/1   Adopted S.T. Meridian 30E00

No Daylight Saving Time

See also Rhodesia

ZANZIBAR

British protectorate in Indian Ocean off the eastern coast of Africa. Became independent December 10, 1963.

Capital: Zanzibar 6S10 39E11

By 1931	Observing S.T. Meridian 37E30
Later	Shifted to S.T. Meridian 41E15 (date unknown)
	Shifted to S.T. Meridian 45E00 (1940s?)

See also Tanzania

ZIMBABWE

Located in East Africa. Became independent April 18, 1980

Capital: Harare (Salisbury) 17S50 31E03

Standard Time Meridian: 30E00 No Daylight Savings Time

ZULULAND See Union of South Africa

Recent release of Russian time changes from Valadimir Karpinsky of Moscow.

Time changes in the USSR territory

Date & time (hh,mm)	Time shift (hh,mm)	Comments	Time equivalent to Greenwich (for Moscow)
(Time standard 30e01)			
01/07/1917 23:00	+01:00	Russia, summer time: start	−03:31
28/12/1917 00:00	−01:00	RSFSR, summer time: end	−02:31
31/05/1918 22:00	+02:00	RSFSR, summer time: start	−04:31
17/09/1918 00:00	−01:00	RSFSR, summer time: end	−03:31
31/05/1919 23:00	+01:00	RSFSR, summer time: start	−04:31
*01/07/1919 02:00		RSFSR, zone time: start	−04:00
16/08/1919 00:00	−01:00	RSFSR, summer time: end	−03:00
14/02/1921 23:00	+01:00	RSFSR, summer time: start	−04:00
20/03/1921 23:00	+01:00	RSFSR, summer time: start	−05:00
01/09/1921 00:00	−01:00	RSFSR, summer time: end	−04:00
01/10/1921 00:00	−01:00	RSFSR, summer time: end	−03:00
01/10/1922 00:00	−01:00	RSFSR, summer time: end	−02:00
02/05/1924 00:00		USSR, zone time was established	−02:00
(Time standard 45e00)			
21/06/1930 00:00	+01:00	USSR, decree time was established	−03:00
*01/03/1957 00:00		USSR, time zones were changed	
*01/04/1981 00:00	+01:00	USSR, summer time: start	−04:00
01/10/1981 00:00	−01:00	USSR, summer time: end	−03:00
*01/04/1982 00:00	+01:00	USSR, summer time: start	−04:00
01/10/1982 00:00	−01:00	USSR, summer time: end	−03:00
01/04/1983 00:00	+01:00	USSR, summer time: start	−04:00
01/10/1983 00:00	−01:00	USSR, summer time: end	−03:00
01/04/1984 00:00	+01:00	USSR, summer time: start	−04:00
30/09/1984 03:00	−01:00	USSR, summer time: end	−03:00
31/03/1985 02:00	+01:00	USSR, summer time: start	−04:00
29/09/1985 03:00	−01:00	USSR, summer time: end	−03:00
30/03/1986 02:00	+01:00	USSR, summer time: start	−04:00
28/09/1986 03:00	−01:00	USSR, summer time: end	−03:00
29/03/1987 02:00	+01:00	USSR, summer time: start	−04:00
27/09/1987 03:00	−01:00	USSR, summer time: end	−03:00
*27/03/1988 02:00	+01:00	USSR, summer time: start	−04:00
25/09/1988 03:00	−01:00	USSR, summer time: end	−03:00
*26/03/1989 02:00	+01:00	USSR, summer time: start	−04:00
24/09/1989 03:00	−01:00	USSR, summer time: end	−03:00
*25/03/1990 02:00	+01:00	USSR, summer time: start	−04:00
*30/09/1990 03:00	−01:00	USSR, summer time: end	−03:00
31/03/1991 02:00	+01:00	USSR, summer time: start	−04:00
30/09/1991 03:00	−01:00	USSR, summer time: end	−03:00

(*) - Time zones were changed